Las Vegas Travel Tips
2015

M. J. Veaudry

By M. J. Veaudry

Cover Image by M. J. Veaudry

Copyright 2013 - 2015 M. J. Veaudry

ISBN - 13: 9781491035375
ISBN - 10: 1491035374

Dedication

I would like to dedicate this book to everyone who, over the last thirty years, asked me about what to do and see in Las Vegas. You know who you are. You were the inspiration for this book.

I would particularly like to thank my loving wife who suffered through the writing, re-writing, proofreading, the artwork and expletives along the way. This book could not have been written without her support and encouragement.

While I tried very hard to correct all possible errors (grammar, spelling, punctuation, you name it), there are just so many times you can read the same material.

Any errors remaining are entirely my responsibility and if you find any, I apologize in advance and hope you will forgive me.

M. J. Veaudry

Contents

1.0 Introduction

I have been coming to Las Vegas since 1984. I bought property here in 1994 and over the last 30 years have seen incredible changes to the city and the area.

Friends and relatives are always asking me for information on what to see and do on their visit to Las Vegas. I got asked this so often that I decided to write it down.

Las Vegas Travel Tips is a witty, easy to read book about 100 pages long that describes the best that Vegas has to offer. It will cover only what you need to know to get around and enjoy the city. I have personally selected everything in the book so when there are several options for you to chose from you can be assured that whichever one you pick you will not be disappointed.

There are no endorsements; no one has paid me to promote a particular attraction, tour, show or restaurant.

Since Las Vegas is constantly changing, I have included specific website references so you can get the most current information before you go. These are set apart from the rest of the text using the following format and spacing:

www.url (uniform resource locator).com.

Enter the hyperlink (the line above) into your web browser to go to the web page specified in the url address. It is that easy. This feature alone will save you hours of searching the web. You will also get the most current information.

This book is not about gambling.

It is intended for people who want to see more of Las Vegas than the inside of a casino. You may be with friends or a companion that likes to gamble but you are not sure what to do on your own. The book is filled with great suggestions that will keep you busy while they gamble.

Las Vegas Travel Tips is focused on getting the best value for your dollar while maximizing your entertainment value. This is particularly true in today's economy. While you can find terrific reductions in airfares, hotel accommodations and packages to Las Vegas you do not see any great reduction in the cost of shows, tours, shopping, dining or attractions. There are, of course, some deals to be had and I will point these out as you read the book.

Viva Las Vegas

2.0 Getting Started

So you want to go to Las Vegas. This may be your first trip or you may simply be going back. Regardless, you will want to get the most out of your trip. Friends may have told you about their trip and where they stayed and what they did. Nevertheless, you should be aware of a few basic things that will make your visit a great trip.

If you have been before you can probably skip most of this chapter. However, even seasoned visitors to Las Vegas will want to make sure they don't schedule their visit during a large convention or trade show. Everyone should read: *"When is the best time to go?"*

2.1 Some things to keep in mind

Everyone knows that economic times are tough and I am sure you have noticed the deep discounts for airfares to Las Vegas and accommodation while in Las Vegas. Some hotels are even offering free rooms on certain days of the month. While this is all very well for the visitor don't be fooled into thinking that everything in Vegas has been discounted. This simply has not happened.

For example, taxi fares have increased and bus fares have doubled in the last few years. You can expect them to continue to rise to pay for the new buses running on the Strip and the continued increase in gasoline prices. Check the fare before you get on the bus (you will need the exact change). The fares are posted on the route signs at each stop and are subject to change without notice. A 24-hour pass is still the best ticket to buy. You can purchase it at the kiosk (found at most stops) or on the bus (again correct change is necessary). You may also buy multiple tickets from the driver as long as you have the correct change for the total amount. For example, if the price of one 24-hour ticket is $8 (a $5 bill and three $1 bills) you can buy two 24-hour tickets for $16 (three $5 bills and one $1 bill).

Check out the current fares at:

www.rtcsouthernnevada.com

by clicking on TRANSIT Ride with Us.

Meals are also increasing in price. Although the price of meals continues to increase year-over-year, properties are trying to attract visitors with specials linked to their loyalty cards. For example, Caesars Entertainment Corporation offers a 24-hour buffet pass called "Buffet of Buffets" that's good at six of its Las Vegas properties (Paris, Caesars Palace, Harrah's, Planet Hollywood, Flamingo and Rio). You can also mix and match. You don't have to eat at the same property. You can buy the pass at any of the properties and it is good for 24-hours from the time of purchase. If you buy the pass at a late dinner one night you should be able to get a breakfast, lunch and an early dinner in the next day within the 24-hour limit. Check the price out at any of the participating properties before you arrive.

Also note that there is an extra charge for using Caesars Palace or the Rio (so watch the fine print). What was a great deal when it first came out is now only a good deal.

Check out the other properties for buffet deals as well. Luxor and Excalibur offer the Take 2 Buffet Pass for a lot less than the Buffet of Buffet Pass. You need to be aware that the buffet at the Excalibur is undergoing a renovation and will probably not reopen until February.

Shows and Attractions are also increasing in price. A 20% increase year-over-year is also not uncommon now. It is even more important now to look for ticket discounts before you come and when you arrive. In the section on *"Entertainment"* I will discuss this in more detail.

It appears to me that while the resorts and casinos are very interested in making it attractive for you to come to Las Vegas they don't have the same incentive in reducing your expenses once you get here. In fact, they have raised the cost of some things downtown and on the Strip to try and increase their profits to make up for the decline during the last few years while attendance was lower. This does not seem like a good long-term strategy to me and may backfire on them. I'll let you be the judge of this.

To offset this increase in costs most casino/resorts are offering more discount coupons than usual and many of these are handed out on the street in front of the property (not to be confused with the other people snapping cards in front of the property to get your attention). If you look for these coupons you will enjoy some savings.

Because costs are going up I am making the following recommendations.

Only buy discounted show tickets (see the *"Entertainment"* chapter on how and where to get these).

Buy discounted dining vouchers (see the *"Dining Out"* chapter on how and where to get these).

Consider sharing a meal (portion sizes are large and while most places now have an extra plate charge, it is still well worth it – you eat less, feel better and save money). There is no shame in sharing. More people are doing it. It's why restaurants now charge you for the extra plate.

2.2 When is the best time to go?

This depends a lot on what you plan to do. Most of my friends like it when it is warm enough to swim in the outdoor pools (April – September). Since most pools are no longer heated and the evenings are cold in October – March you can't always count on using a pool in these months. In the winter months a lot of the pools are closed anyway.

My favorite time of the year is April and September. The weather is great and the kids are still in school. If you're interested in doing the eco tours they also run in this timeframe.

I was recently reminded of some things the locals take for granted in Las Vegas when we had friends visit us in September who came to Las Vegas for the first time. They wanted to do and see as much as they could in the week they spent with us so we had a pretty busy itinerary. On the third day however one of our friends got ill and it took her a couple of days to recover. We suspect she had heat stoke (the week they were here the average temperature was 105 degrees – unusually warm for late September). She was also not drinking enough water and probably became dehydrated. So the lesson for everyone is simple – Las Vegas is in the desert, it's usually hot, so pace yourself, drink lots of water, wear a hat and cover yourself in sun block and moisturizer. A good moisturizer is very important since your skin can dry out very quickly. Be sure to apply it 2 or 3 times a day.

If you plan to hit the shows, shopping and casinos then anytime is a good time since these activities are almost always indoors. The only caution I would give you is to try and avoid the time when there are major conventions or trade shows going on.

Las Vegas hosts a number of very large conferences each year and while the attendees may not spend a lot of time in the casinos they and their companions certainly fill up the restaurants, shows and shopping malls.

Even though the cost of a hotel room has dropped significantly there are still blackout times to compensate for when a large conference is in town and the vacancy rate is low. These are the times you want to avoid.

You can get a complete list of the current conventions and trade shows that are planned at:

www.vegasmeansbusiness.com.

Just click SEARCH on the Convention Calendar and enter the start date and end date you want to travel on to view a full list of the conventions and shows planned for that time period.

Don't be discouraged by the large number of events. Some of these are very small and specialized venues. Check for the number of expected attendees (shown at the end of each conference). You may want to avoid going whenever there is a convention or trade show with more than 100,000 attendees. The National Association of Broadcasters meets in April each year and has about 100,000 delegates. The International Consumer Electronics Show, one of the largest convention and trade shows in Vegas (usually held in early January) has drawn over 150,000 attendees. Don't forget a lot of these attendees will also show up with a significant other, so if you think you can just plan your activities around their conferences – think again.

While there is no doubt that the number and size of conferences are shrinking as a result of the economy, you should still check before you go. Don't forget, some of these trade shows and conferences are booked over a year in advance.

2.3 How long should I stay?

This depends on how much time and money you have to spend. Remember, Las Vegas is the entertainment capital of the world and like all entertainment you must expect to pay for it.

Most people come to Las Vegas for a mini-vacation – these usually run from Sunday – Thursday or Thursday – Sunday. Most packages (hotel and airfare) are offered for these days. The Thursday – Sunday timeframe has the advantage that it makes better use of your weekend and you only lose two workdays. The disadvantage of these dates is that Las Vegas is usually busier at the end of the week and on weekends than it is during the early part of the week. Hotel rates are also more expensive on the weekends.

With the airlines now quoting one-way fares, you may decide to go for a week. This is my recommendation. This takes a lot of the stress off you for trying to pack a lot into a short time and allows you to see Vegas in a much more relaxed manner.

2.4 Where are the best places to stay?

This is the question that I get asked the most. However, it is the wrong question to ask. People will stay at a hotel that fits their budget and that's the bottom line. There are almost 2 million web sites with the key words Las Vegas and most of these would be pleased to provide you airfare and a hotel room on the Strip. I am not going to compete with these sites and I would prefer to leave it up to you and your pocketbook to sort this one out. If you want to browse a few of these sites, try:

www.travelocity.com or www.priceline.com.

These are both excellent sites.

Rates have dropped significantly for the four/five star resorts, so treat yourself and stay at one of them. There are great deals on right now at CityCenter, so try Vdara, Mandarin Oriental, Aria or the Cosmopolitan for something really different. My favorites are Bellagio, Venetian and Wynn so you have lots to choose from.

If you don't have a hotel preference, you might consider staying at one of the many timeshare properties on the Strip. There are more timeshare units in Las Vegas than any other city in the world. These units are family friendly, high quality, most have a small kitchen and are often less expensive than hotel rooms. Since many visitors have not discovered the advantages of staying in a timeshare unit there are plenty of properties to choose from. Also remember that you have no obligation to take a timeshare presentation. One of the best advantages is that you can stock the unit with breakfast supplies so you don't have to worry about getting up and out for breakfast each day. Just lounge around, enjoy a leisurely breakfast in your own room while reading the newspaper. This is much more relaxing than trying to find somewhere to get breakfast.

You can buy most breakfast supplies at any CVS Pharmacy. These are scattered up and down the Strip. For $25 you will be able to feed two people for a week. This alone will save you about $200 in food cost. Check out the map reference below to find out where the timeshare units are, then google the property to find the price and amenities they offer. I think you will be pleasantly surprised.

My recommendation is to choose a place to stay based on its location and not a particular property. Anywhere on the Strip between the Venetian at one end and Planet Hollywood at the other end would be a prime location to stay. I call this the Center Strip area. The hotels that fan out from the intersection of S. Las Vegas Blvd. and E. Flamingo Rd. are in the best location. For a complete list of the hotels and timeshare units in this area you can google *Las Vegas Strip Map* in your web browser.

If you stay in this area you will find it an easy walk to get from hotel to hotel without relying on surface transportation. The Las Vegas Strip is often very congested and it can take a long time to go even a short distance. Please see the section on *"Getting Around".*

As you move out from this location there are still a lot of very good hotels. If you decide to stay further up or down the Strip or you are unable to get accommodation in this area you should be prepared to take surface transportation to get around. I will deal with the pros and cons of different types of transport on the Strip in the *"Getting Around"* section.

People may tell you that they prefer to stay downtown on Fremont Street. I know a lot of older people like this destination. There are a lot of hotel/casinos in this relatively small area. This makes it very easy to move from one casino to another by just crossing Fremont Street. This is made even easier due to the fact that Fremont Street between Las Vegas Blvd. and Main Street is a pedestrian mall and home to the Fremont Street Experience. The flip side to this is that the hotels/casinos are older and smaller than what you will find on the Strip. If you were visiting Las Vegas for the first time, I would avoid staying at the downtown hotels unless you have a disability that would make it difficult for you to get around on the Strip.

2.5 What should I wear?

Las Vegas is very informal. You will see people wearing almost anything at any venue.

I've seen a six-foot tall dominatrix, yes in leather, pulling a slave behind her, complete with collar, across the crowded predestination overpass between New York - New York and MGM Grand. This turned a few heads, I can tell you.

Generally, however, restaurants will require you to wear shoes and a shirt to get service. In the evening at some of the best nightspots and restaurants you may be asked to wear a shirt with a collar or even a jacket but this is very rare and usually done by choice.

For evening shows some people will dress-up but this is entirely up to you. Most people will come in whatever they were wearing that day. For playing in the casino, informal wear is very acceptable. Just use common sense and you should be fine.

The chart below shows the average temperatures by month:

Month	Hi	Low
January	57	34
February	63	34
March	69	44
April	78	51
May	88	60
June	100	69
July	106	76
August	103	74
September	95	66
October	82	54
November	67	42
December	58	34

Las Vegas is in the desert and it will get cooler when the sun goes down so plan accordingly. In the winter months (Dec. – Feb.) when it may be wetter and cooler during the day you might even want to wear a light jacket.

2.6 Finding the best discounts

There are many places to get discounts for Las Vegas. You don't have to do this but I had an uncle whose favorite saying was "only a schmuck pays retail". He was in the garment industry so I think he knew what he was talking about. In any case there are numerous discounts available for Las Vegas and here are a few of the more popular ways to get them. After all, every penny you save off the retail price is more money you have to spend on shopping. Am I right or am I right?

Before going to Las Vegas

There are a number of things you can do before you go to Las Vegas to ensure you get the best discounts possible in Las Vegas. This will require a little effort on your part but it will pay dividends in the form of some excellent discounts when you get there.

ly know about Groupon then pay attention. e fastest growing sites on the Internet. Once ו by going to their site at:

..w.groupon.com

you will be asked to sign up for a Groupon account. Enter your full name, email address and a password. Select Las Vegas, use the zip code 89109 for the Las Vegas strip. They will then send you a deal each day that can be redeemed for events in that city – neat or what?

Each deal will have terms and conditions (called Fine Print) associated with it, so read these carefully. In most cases they will have an expiry date and in some cases there will be a limit on the number of deals available so you may have to act quickly. If you find one you want to buy just click the BUY button and provide your billing information and credit card information. Groupon will email you the coupon complete with a bar code. You can print the Groupon and bring it with you to activate it or you can download it to your mobile device and activate it electronically (just bring up the bar code and they will scan it electronically) when you're ready to use the coupon.

If the deal does not get enough subscribers then the deal will be cancelled. But don't worry, they will ask you if you want a credit for it or if you want to add it to your account against future deals. They do this quickly and I have never had a problem getting a credit when this happens, which isn't often.

Some of the deals I have seen include;
• $49 (61% off) for The V Card ultimate nightlife-pass to access some of Vegas' hippest nightclubs, adult cabarets, lounges and bars,
• $19 (52%) off the Las Vegas Mob Experience,
• $35 (52%) off V The Ultimate Variety Show,
• $25 for a $50 gift certificate at the Golden Steer Steakhouse,

• $15 (67%) off Echoes of the 60's at the V Theater.

Groupon will send you a new deal each day and when your trip is completed just click "unsubscribe" on the next deal you get emailed and they will stop sending you any for Las Vegas. This is a fun way to get some good discounts. I recommend that you sign up for Groupon for Las Vegas at least three weeks before you go so you get to see the best deals during your visit.

They also encourage you to share the deals with your friends and others who may be traveling with you to Las Vegas. So as they say, get your "Group On".

Online Sites
In addition to Groupon there are also websites that you can visit to get the latest coupons or promo codes for Las Vegas deals. Some of the sites I like to use are:

www.earlyvegas.com,
www.smartervegas.com and
www.vegas.com.

All of these sites will offer you great discounts on hotels, shows, dining, tours and attractions. If you are planning a trip to Las Vegas take a few moments and check these sites out.

The site vegas.com (above) has excellent discounts and I have always been delighted with how professional their service has been. They will often bundle together a show and dinner at an excellent price. Make sure you check them out before your trip. You will be able to purchase the tickets in advance of your trip and they will send you an email with the confirmation number you will take to the box office to get your ticket. One of their recent deals was to purchase the lowest general admission ticket for Rita Rudner and you would get an upgrade to the best available seat in the house. We ended up in row C left of center (excellent seats) for about 65% off the list price.

The Bite Card

This is a relatively new card that is being offered with discounts on shows, nightclubs, spas, food, golf and weddings. As the card becomes more popular the number of merchants accepting the card will undoubtedly increase. The idea behind the card is that you purchase it for one year and it has unlimited usage until the card expires, so you can use it over multiple trips.

You only need to present the card to get the discounts. No identification is required so you can share the card with your friends. It's that simple. You can buy the card online and get free shipping or pick it up on the Strip. Just make sure you do not lose the card because they will not replace it.

The number of merchants accepting the card is always changing so you are advised to check out their web site for the current merchants:

www.vegasbitecard.com.

When the card was first introduced the price of the card was $34.95. If you plan to use these merchants it is an excellent purchase.

When you are in Las Vegas

If you are not comfortable in making purchases on the Internet you can always find discounted tickets when you get there. While there are many people who would like to sell you cheap tickets on the Strip you must be careful. Check the date and time to make sure it isn't for a past performance. Yes, I know people who have fallen for this one. The suggestions below are from reputable sources. I have used all of them and they give great service.

24/7 Magazine

The easiest way to get discounted tickets is to pickup the small magazine (24/7) that you will find in the cab behind the driver's seat. This little book fits easily in your pocket so you can carry it around with you and it is full of discount coupons. The magazine is published every month and it will cover the month of your visit. It includes a wealth of information, coupons and a good listing of shows, headliners, restaurants, nightclubs, tours, shopping and anything else going on in Las Vegas during your visit.

Frequently there is a 2 for 1 coupon for Jubilee (playing at Bally's). These coupons are not in every issue of the magazine so check to see if your issue has them. Use this information to identify the shows, tours and dining experiences you'd like to see and do during your visit.

TIX4TONIGHT

There are many people on the Strip who will offer you discounted tickets but I prefer to use TIX4TONIGHT. You can check them out on the Internet at their website:

www.tix4tonight.com.

They now have many convenient locations in Las Vegas – including the Fashion Show Mall (Strip entrance in front of Neiman Marcus), Circus Circus (on the north end of the Strip outside Circus Circus), Downtown (the Four Queens Hotel at the Fremont Street Experience), Hawaiian Marketplace (the South Strip at the Polo Towers), Showcase Mall (South Strip at the base of the giant Coke bottle and the newly opened one right next to the MGM Grand), Bally's (just outside the casino and steps away from Paris), Planet Hollywood (just in front of the resort) and Casino Royale (right next to Denny's and across the street from the Mirage) in addition to other new locations that they are always opening. You are sure to find an outlet somewhere close to where you are staying.

Once you know what shows you are looking for just visit one of their locations, decide on a show (tickets are usually for the same day although they might have advance sales – means tomorrow) and buy the voucher. They do not sell you the actual ticket but you get a voucher that you then have to take to the theater and exchange for the specific ticket(s) before the show.

When you purchase your ticket you will be given a choice of sections to choose from. I always pick the cheapest section. The reason for this is simple – all theaters have good seats (long gone are the days of being seated behind a pillar because you didn't tip the usher) and while the attendance remains down many of the theaters will move you to better seats. For this reason always come at the last minute. They have a better idea then of what seats and sections are not filled. Often they will tell you that your seat has been changed when you enter the theater. It doesn't always happen, but it does happen often enough that you should try it.

The last two shows I saw, I bought the general admission ticket and when we went to the theater for the performance they upgraded us to the VIP section. As long as attendance is down you can expect this to happen more frequently. So don't be too quick to upgrade your ticket when the theater box office tries to up sell you or later when you get a text or email from the theater (usually just before the show) to get an upgrade at a discount price. Hang tough and wait for the free upgrade when you enter the theater. It's worth the wait.

The other thing I often do is go to pickup my ticket for a late show (say 10:00 pm) about an hour before the earlier show (say 7:00 pm). Ask the clerk if you can get into the earlier show instead of waiting for the late show. If they have the space they will usually try to accommodate you and often you will get a better seat than the one you purchased.

The line-up at TIX4TONIGHT can be long. You need to know that if you keep your receipt and your ticket stub you will be able to return the next day and go through the VIP line (usually no waiting). The VIP line is only good if you return within 24 hours. However, some locations are less crowded than others. If you can, use the location outside Circus Circus. This location is usually not crowded at all and I have never had to wait in line.

You might also consider printing off the coupon on their website before going to Las Vegas. It will save you $2.00 on each ticket for up-to 4 tickets in your party. You should also be aware that popular shows, like "O" are almost always sold out so tickets for these shows are not usually discounted or available at TIX4TONIGHT.

TIX4DINNER

TIX4TONIGHT also offers a large range of discount dinner tickets. Just go to their website or visit one of their convenient locations on the Strip and select a dinning choice. You get to them online by clicking on TIX4DINNER at the top of their home page. They offer up to a 50% discount on some restaurants but you can expect to save at least 25%.

So if you are looking for a show and want something special for dinner just ask them about TIX4DINNER when you get the TIX4TONIGHT show voucher. They can even make the dinner reservation for you while you wait.

On the Street

Also pay attention to the people on the street who are offering you coupons for anything from free afternoon shows to free appetizers with an entrée. You can usually pickup free tickets for the auto show outside the Quad in addition to any number of afternoon shows where you get a free ticket as long as you buy two drinks from the bar. These drinks will usually cost you $9.99 (total) but remember the show is also included. If you're looking for someplace out of the afternoon heat, this can be an inexpensive way to keep cool.

Timesharing Presentations

It is hard to walk a block in Las Vegas without someone saying, "where are you from", "how long are you in town for" or "would you like a free show". These are all phrases used by people trying to get you to attend a timeshare presentation. Not everyone wants to spend his or her vacation time taking a timeshare presentation. But Las Vegas has more timeshares than any other city in the world. So you should expect to meet these people in Las Vegas. You can simply ignore them and keep on walking or you can stop, negotiate a reward for your time and signup for a presentation.

You can expect them to offer you a free show for two, free buffet tickets, cash vouchers for free slot play or vouchers for dinning out. Whatever they offer you, don't be shy and ask for more. Ask for two shows or tickets for four if you have friends with you. Times are tough so make sure you get as much as you can for your time.

If you do decide on the presentation be prepared to spend at least two hours with them. They will tell you an hour is all they need but it will be longer. If you show any real interest in what they are selling it could take a lot longer. My rule of thumb is to say very little and keep your answers to one word or less.

Signing Up For Loyalty Cards
Even if you do not plan to gamble, it is still a good idea to pick up loyalty cards. Just for signing up you might get a free buffet or show for two. Also, by signing up you will get email from them telling you about any specials they might have that you can use for a future trip.

The other thing you should know about Loyalty Cards is that you get a better deal when you first signup for one than when you are returning and have one already. Check before you enter the casino to see if they are handing out these coupons on the street. Unfortunately, these coupons usually apply to new members only.

If you already have loyalty cards you should drop by the appropriate rewards centers and ask if your card's points are still good. Most of the loyalty programs will keep your points for one year but they will keep you on file for several years so in all likelihood you will only be able to become a new member once. So just signup you or your traveling companion this trip and signup the other one the next trip unless you have a really good offer (like a show or a buffet) for signing up. There is usually no really good advantage for signing both of you up at the same time.

Also, ask for two cards when you sign up. Keep one card for yourself and give the other one to your companion. This way you will both be able to use the same card and you will accumulate points much faster. If you have more people in your party get each of them a card. This will really rack up the points. This is important because the comps awarded to the card will increase as more points are accumulated.

Exchanging Vouchers for Tickets

When you get your voucher, coupon, ticket or whatever you will need to exchange it for an actual theater ticket at the show's box office.

My recommendation is to take any vouchers or coupons you have purchased in advance or at TIX4TONIGHT and go to the theater box office as early as you can to select your seats. Groupon, TIX4TONIGHT or Vegas.com will tell you that you only need to pickup your tickets one hour before the performance but the earlier you make the seat selection the better the seat you will get. I often go to the box office several days in advance to pick my seat. You may want to do the same thing.

3.0 Welcome to Las Vegas

The first thing you will notice when you get off the plane is that there are slot machines at the airport. The win percentage is lower on these machines than any other machines in Las Vegas. There are two things you never do at an airport – play slot machines or get a haircut. In both cases they do not expect repeat business and they treat you accordingly.

After you've claimed your luggage and if you are not renting a car, proceed directly to the taxi stand. The lineups can be long depending on the time and day you arrive and the terminal you come into but they move quickly and it is still the best way to get to your hotel. You may be tempted by other modes of transportation – but my recommendation is to take a cab. It's worth the money. The taxi drivers in Las Vegas love to talk. Like the rest of the service industry in Vegas, they too are working hard for your tip. They will answer any questions you might have and don't be afraid to ask them what's new in Vegas. You should also know that cab drivers in Las Vegas are obliged to take you to your destination by the most direct route. If they ask you if you want to go via the highway or any specific route just tell them you want to go the most direct way. This will save you time and money.

One of the advantages of taking the taxi is that on the seat behind the driver is a pouch with a free pocket sized magazine called 24/7. Take one for yourself and everyone traveling with you. The magazine is published every month and it will cover the month of your visit. It includes a wealth of information, some coupons and a good listing of shows, headliners, restaurants, nightclubs, tours, shopping and anything else going on in Las Vegas during your visit. Besides, it's small and can easily fit into your pocket. What more could you want?

If you are planning to rent a car, just hop on any of the blue and white shuttle buses that are always going by. McCarran International Airport has a Rent-A-Car Center where all rental car companies are located. These buses will take you to the Rent-A-Car Center located three miles from the airport at 7135 Gilespie Street. Once there, just follow the crowd, go inside and look for your rental car company. The Rent-A-Car Center is easy to find and the directions are well marked when you are returning the car. Similarly, it is also easy to get out of and close to the highway.

3.1 Getting Oriented

The Las Vegas Strip is four (4) miles long and runs from Mandalay Bay in the south to the Stratosphere in the north. It is best if you think of the Strip in three sections – South, Center and North.

The South Strip is located at Las Vegas Blvd. and Tropicana Ave. The Tropicana, Excalibur, New York - New York and MGM Grand are located at this intersection.

The Center Strip is located at Las Vegas Blvd. and Flamingo Rd. Bally's, Bellagio, Caesars Palace and the Flamingo are located at this intersection. The newly complete boutique hotel/casino The Cromwell has replaced Bill's Gamblin' Hall & Saloon and is also located on this corner.

The North Strip is located at Las Vegas Blvd. and Riviera Blvd. The Riviera and Circus Circus are located at this intersection.

There are of course many other hotel/casinos near these intersections and between them.

On the South Strip, the Tropicana, acquired by Double Tree (Hilton), has completed a $200 million upgraded. The rooms are freshly decorated and the pool has been voted the best Las Vegas pool.

The Center Strip is by far the most popular area and with the opening of the CityCenter this will continue to be the trend for the next few years.

Despite the efforts to remove the ill-fated Harmon by implosion, it will now be peeled away floor by floor until nothing is left of the building that was once to be the front door of CityCentre. The structurally flawed 26 story condo and hotel will probably not be totally demolished until the Fall of 2015.

The courts are still fussing over how much time insurance carrier GM Global needs to investigate the Harmon's defects to decide the amount of CityCenter's $394 million claim it will pay.

The Linq, the newly created outdoor mall, situated in what was the driveway between the Quad (aka Imperial Palace) and the Flamingo is now open. There are 40 shops and restaurants in a 300,000 square foot area. The High Roller (the world's tallest observation wheel at 550 feet) is located at the end of the promenade offers 360 degree spectacular views of the Las Vegas valley. The venues include; O'Sheas, Haute Doggery, Koto Shop,

Yard House, Goorin Brothers, Polaroid Fotobar, Chilli Beans, F.A.M.E., Sprinkles, Vanity Style Loungs, Flour & Barley, Tilted Kilt, Ghirardelli, ALLO! MON COCO, 12A.M. Run, The Stomping Grape, Ruby Blue, Off the Strip, Bella Scarpa, Chayo Mexicano, Brooklyn Bowl plus many more.

On the North Strip, after a $415 million renovation, the SLS (aka Sahara) opened its doors Aug. 23, 2014. But don't expect much to be the same. An ultramodern look and style with elements reminiscent of Hollywood Boulevard and the Sunset Strip. The pool has been rebuilt, an additional rooftop pool added atop a party tower, the Alexandria Tower will become all suites, the monorail entrance has already been torn down and rebuilt for easier accessibility, the lobby has been revamped, the NASCAR cafe and Congo Showroom have been morphed into clubs and much more.

The Malaysia based Genting Group bought the Echelon parcel (87 acres formerly occupied by the Stardust) for $350 million and plan to incorporate much of what Boyd had planned in the new $2 billion - $7 billion Resorts World Las Vegas. There is no timeframe on when this might come online but the local chatter is it will not be until 2016 or 2017.

In future years, these two areas in particular, will become more developed and will help to redefine the North Strip.

3.2 Getting Around

Walking

If you were able to find accommodation in the Center Strip it is easy to visit a number of world-class hotels/casinos including (but not limited to) the Venetian, TI (Treasure Island), Mirage, Caesars Palace, Bellagio, Paris and PH (Planet Hollywood) by just walking around. This will always be the quickest way to move around the Center Strip.

The Las Vegas Strip is over 4 miles long and it is not recommended that you try to walk the entire Strip. However, walking is still the preferred way to explore the South Strip (hotels located close to the intersection of Las Vegas Blvd and Tropicana), the Center Strip (hotels located close to the intersection of Las Vegas Blvd and Flamingo Rd.), the North Strip (hotels located close to the intersection of Las Vegas Blvd and Riviera Blvd.) and Downtown Las Vegas (hotels located on or near the Fremont St. Experience).

If you are walking it is very important to obey traffic signals and walk only when the signal indicates. If you cannot make it all of the way across the street on a green light then you can stop on the median in the middle of the road and wait for the next light. There is usually a countdown with the walk sign so you will know exactly how many seconds you have to make it to the other side. But be warned, you will have to move at a quick pace to get across the street as the time to cross the street is often very short. Every week, tourists driving cars hit other tourists looking at the sights and crossing against the traffic lights. Don't become a statistic. If possible use the overhead pedestrian walkways – they are there for a reason.

When walking on the Las Vegas Strip there are people paid to hand out pamphlets and magazines with pictures or ads for sex that may be objectionable to you. They will try to get your attention by snapping their fingers or thrusting the ads at you. Do not hold out your hand to take them, the people that are giving them away will not bother or harass you in any way if you ignore them. Legally they are not allowed to interfere with you in anyway.

Some hotels like Bellagio own the side walks so they are private property and you will not be accosted when you walk in front of these properties. The older properties however do not own the sidewalks that are therefore public property. These are the locations where most of these people gather.

Las Vegas is, generally speaking, a very safe city. Police patrol the busier sections of the Strip on bicycles. The hotels/casinos have their own security so if you ever feel threatened in any way just step inside – criminals will not follow you into a casino. However, like any large city Las Vegas is not devoid of crime. Here are some things to keep in mind as you move around.

The Center Strip is the busiest area and the crowds alone provide a large measure of safety. However, the crowds also bring out the pickpockets and you will need to keep your hands on your valuables. I had my pocket picked once and ever since I walk with a hand in the pocket where I carry my money and credit cards. Never carry your valuables (money, wallet etc.) in your back pocket (even if you have a button on it), in a purse slung over your shoulder or a backpack – these are all easy prey for an experienced pickpocket.

Downtown is also very busy, particularly around the pedestrian mall. While traffic is not a big problem here since the street is closed to traffic, pickpockets like to work this area also. If you are downtown at night, stick to Fremont Street. If you wander too far from the Fremont Street Experience you will encounter a seedier part of town and may see drug addicts, drunks and will most likely be approached by someone asking for money. This is a side of Las Vegas you should try to avoid.

Electronic scanners have become a very popular way of stealing credit card information without even lifting a victim's credit card. They are used in crowded areas where the thief can simply walk past a crowd with the scanner turned on to pick up all of the credit card data from each victim. Most of these victims will never know that their information has been stolen. At least not until the thief makes a purchase on their card. If you plan to visit Las Vegas and you have a credit card with a radio frequency identification (RFID) capability you should consider buying an RFID wallet. These cards usually have a symbol of a tower with curved lines emanating from it or something that says "easy pay" or anything that implies you can tap the card to male a payment. You can buy these inexpensive wallets at most travel stores. I have even seen them at the dollar store. Use one of these wallets and you might save yourself a lot of grief.

The South Strip is not as well traveled as the Center Strip and Downtown areas but there are still enough people about to make you feel safe. The construction on the Strip at CityCenter is now complete so it is just as easy to walk on either side of the Strip. I usually walk on the side that offers the most shade.

The North Strip however is the least traveled area and you should be very careful when walking here at night. Usually, there are not many people about and it is almost certain that in this area, at night, if you are walking in ones or twos someone will ask you for money. Because of the construction sites in this area there are a number of long barren stretches. This area is also attracting a lot of homeless people. There is usually nothing to fear from them but they can be intimidating. Do not walk in this area after dark or if you do then walk with a group.

If you want to go further a field and you will, then there are four excellent modes of surface transportation available to you (automobiles, taxis, buses and monorail) plus two other less used modes of transportation (free shuttles and other free conveyances). Let's look at each of these in turn.

Automobile Rental

You may have rented a car already and picked it up at the Transportation Center. If you haven't and you want one for a day or longer ask your concierge for the nearest hotel where you can rent a car on the Strip. Car rental agencies have pick up and drop off points at specific hotels so you can check with them before you come to find the closest site to where you are staying.

In addition to the usual car rental agencies there are a number of rentals located on the Las Vegas Strip. These offer high end or unusual vehicles to make your visit more memorable. If you're looking for something different and you want to drive a Ferrari, Lamborghini, Porsche, classic cars like a 1959 Cadillac convertible or a motorcycle check out Dream Car Rentals at:

www.dreamcarrentals.com

with their main location at 5050 Paradise Road, next to the airport. They will also pick you up at your Strip hotel if you call them at (702) 731-6452.

Parking is free at all hotel/casinos. You can park the car yourself in their parking garage (just follow the signs) or leave it with a valet and they will park it for you. If you leave it with the valet you will enter at the hotel entrance but you will be expected to tip the valet. If you park in the garage you will have a longer walk but no tipping. The longer walk may be offset by the fact that when you go to pick up your car you may have a wait for the valet to get it, particularly if a show is getting out at the same time.

If you have a handicap sticker in your windshield you can go to the head of the line at valet parking and they will park your car for free – no tip required. However, it is still expected that you give them a tip. It's hard to get away without tipping people in Las Vegas.

If you avoid the Strip and use Paradise Rd. and the major cross streets (Tropicana, Harmon, Flamingo, Spring Mountain Rd and Sahara) to get around you can make good time between hotels and since parking is always at the rear of the hotel you can easily avoid entering and leaving the hotel from the Strip that is always busy.

Taxis

Taxis are plentiful in Las Vegas but trying to flag one down on the Strip is a waste of time. However, you can always pick up a cab at the entrance to any hotel on the Strip. There may be a line-up depending on the time of day but generally they move quickly.

The Nevada Taxicab Authority regulates taxi fares in Las Vegas and as such all fares among companies operating in the Las Vegas valley will be the same. The rates below are per carload (up to five people) and not per person. Also, drivers are not allowed to alter from the most direct route. So if the driver asks you if you want to go via a particular way be wary and tell him you want to go via the most direct route. If you think the driver has taken you for a ride and the fares are much higher than those below then ask the hotel valet for help when the taxi pulls up to your destination. The valet will usually speak with the driver and get your fare reduced since most taxi drivers do not want to be put on notice with the Taxi Authority. If this happens to you, remember to tip the valet – not the taxi driver.

From McCarran Airport the approximate fares are (depending on the time of day and traffic conditions):

Taxis Fares from McCarran Airport
South Strip Tropicana, MGM, New York - New York, Excalibur $12.00 - $14.00
Center Strip Bellagio, Bally's, Flamingo, Caesars Palace $14.00 - $16.00
North Strip
Stratosphere, Riviera, Circus Circus
$16.00 - $19.00
Downtown
$21.00 - $24.00

These fares are always changing; particularly based on the current price of gas, so go to the following link to find the current fares from the airport to most hotels:

www.lasvegas-how-to.com/taxi-fare.php.

Buses

The CAT (Citizens Area Transit) is the Las Vegas public transit system. The two routes that most Las Vegas visitors will be concerned with are the Deuce (a double decker bus) that runs the Strip from Mandalay Bay in the south to the Fremont Street Experience in the north and the Downtown Express (SDX) an express bus that makes 16 stops (8 on the Strip) and runs from the South Strip Transfer Terminal (south of Mandalay Bay) to Las Vegas Premium Outlets - North. The Deuce stops at most hotel/

casinos on the Strip making 28 stops and runs between Mandalay Bay and the Fremont Street Experience. At each bus stop there is a route map and on the Strip it will show the stops for both the SDX and the Deuce. Pay careful attention to the stops that are shared so you know the fastest route to take to your destination.

The SDX and Deuce are modern and comfortable buses. Passengers can now buy their tickets at most bus stops to make it even quicker to load. You can buy a 2, 24 and 72 hour ticket. You can also buy your ticket on the bus but you will need the exact change. If two or more of you are traveling together you can purchase multiple tickets with the correct change. So make sure you are carrying the requisite number of small bills before you get on the bus. Bus drivers do not carry cash so they cannot make change. Bus fares are going up as fast as the price of gas at the pump. So ask someone at a bus stop what the current fare is so you can be prepared before you get on the bus. My suggestion is to buy a 24 hr. ticket because it gives you the most flexibility. You can also check the current bus fares at:

www.rtcsnv.com/transit/fare-information/.

The bus is an excellent way to move between the South Strip, Center Strip, North Strip and Downtown. The buses are air conditioned, comfortable and frequent enough that you will usually not have a long wait. You also board them right on the Strip. This is an advantage because the buses will pick you up and drop you off at the front of casinos unlike some other forms of transportation. The major drawback with the bus is that it runs up and down the Las Vegas Strip. This is not a problem in the morning or afternoon but in the evening when the Strip becomes very congested the buses can be slow (there is no express lane for buses). So slow in fact that I have, at times, gotten off and walked the Strip faster than the bus can travel it. You will also want to avoid the times when hotel/casino shifts are changing since the buses can become very crowded at these times. There will usually be a shift change at 8:00 am; 4:00 pm and midnight so try to avoid the bus a half an hour before and after these times.

Las Vegas Monorail

The Las Vegas monorail runs from the MGM Grand Hotel in the south to Sahara Ave in the north, making the following stops;

MGM Grand Station,
Bally's/Paris Station,
Flamingo/Caesars Palace Station,
Quad/Harrah's Station,
Las Vegas Convention Center Station,
Las Vegas Hilton Station and
Sahara Station.

It operates 7 days a week from 7:00 am to 2:00 am Monday - Thursday and until 3:00 am Friday – Sunday. Each car on the Monorail holds 72 riders seated and 152 riders standing. The time to ride from one end of the 4 mile long Las Vegas Strip to the other end is approximately 14 - 16 minutes, depending on the speed of loading and unloading passengers. While this might sound quick you should know that Monorail stations are located at the back of casino properties and you will need to navigate your way through the casino and in some cases the parking garage to catch it.

This is often a lot harder than it seems. Casinos, especially large ones, are designed to make it hard for you to get out once you are inside. This shouldn't surprise you since all casinos are competing for your entertainment dollar and the longer they can keep you in their casino the better the chance of getting some of those dollars. If only I had a nickel for every time I played a slot machine while trying to find my way out of a casino. In any event, it may take as long to walk to and from the monorail station, as it would have taken you to walk between stops. This is more likely the case if you are only going one stop.

The only time I take the Monorail is if I am going from one end of the Strip to the other, without stopping, and then I usually buy a 2 ride pass.

The monorail tickets can be purchased at vending machines located inside each station and at station hotels. Monorail tickets are sold as single ride, one day, two day, three day, four day, five day and seven day passes.

Tickets are good for unlimited travel for the period specified. When the ticket is first used at the fare gates, the period begins. The expiration date and time will be stamped on the ticket upon first use. Remember to take the ticket with you when you pass through the gate.

Las Vegas Monorail Ticket Type	Price
Single Ride Ticket Good for one (1) person for one (1) entry/ ride.	5.00
One Day Pass Good for unlimited travel for one person for a consecutive 24 hour period.	12.00
Two Day Pass Good for unlimited travel for one person for a consecutive 48 hour period.	22.00
Three Day Pass Good for unlimited travel for one person for a consecutive 72 hour period.	28.00
Four Day Pass Good for unlimited travel for one person for a consecutive 96 hour period.	36.00
Five Day Pass Good for unlimited travel for one person for a consecutive 120 hour period	43.00
Seven Day Pass Good for unlimited travel for one person for a consecutive 168 hour period.	56.00

If you want to check on the most current Monorail prices before heading off to Las Vegas go to this link:

www.lvmonorail.com.

Free Shuttles

Some hotels provide free shuttles that run between their properties. This is almost always the case when they have one property on the Strip and another off the Strip.

To find out what shuttles are currently in use, go to this location:

www.lasvegas-how-to.com/free-shuttle.php.

All these shuttles are a free service. However, a tip per rider to the driver would be appreciated. One dollar per rider is usually sufficient.

At the time of publication the following free shuttles were available.

Free Shuttles
Rio/Bally's/Paris/Harrah's: take the free Caesars Entertainment shuttle from the Rio to visit other sister properties on the Strip. Pick up locations Rio: Carnival World Buffet entrance Bally's/Paris: Bally's Entrance (side of Flamingo Rd) Harrah's Las Vegas: Shuttle/Bus/Trolley drop off Shuttle Schedule The Rio free shuttle operates 10:00 a.m - 1:00 a.m. daily 7 days a week Pick up times are approximately every 30 minutes from each location (depending on traffic conditions).
Palms Casino Resort offers a daily shuttle service to and from the Forum Shops at Caesars Palace available 11am to 8 pm every half hour (the shuttle departs from the Palms main entrance).
Gold Coast - Orleans - Las Vegas Strip Shuttle buses run between these two properties and the Las Vegas Strip (Las Vegas Blvd. & Flamingo Road), every half hour from 9:00 am and 12:30 am. The buses pick up new passengers every 20-30 minutes. Preference given to Gold Coast guests.

Other Free Conveyances

There are three trams, a monorail (not to be confused with the Las Vegas Monorail) and a moving walkway between these properties on the Strip. All of these conveyances run 24/7. They run every 10 minutes, so the average wait time is about 5 minutes. They usually are not very crowded so sit back and enjoy the ride.

Property	Pick Up Location	Frequency
Mirage/TI	Side of hotel	Tram Every 10 minutes – 24/7
Bellagio/ CityCenter/Monte Carlo	Indoor boarding platforms at the back of the hotels	Tram Every 10 minutes – 24/7
Excalibur/ Mandalay Bay (express southbound)	Above ground at front of casino	Monorail (Not to be confused with the Las Vegas Monorail) Every 10 minutes – 24/7
Mandalay Bay/ Luxor/Excalibur	Above ground at front of casino. Only north bound stops at Luxor. Southbound is direct Excalibur to Mandalay Bay.	Monorail (Not to be confused with the Las Vegas Monorail) Every 10 minutes – 24/7
Excalibur/Luxor	Follow the signs To Luxor	Moving walkway (2nd floor) Continuous

Hop On Hop Off – Open Top Sightseeing

These open top sightseeing buses that you may have seen in many other cities are now available in Las Vegas. They are particularly popular in European capitals and my wife and I have found them very informative and a great way to get around when you don't know the city.

However, I was very disappointed in the Las Vegas offering. The sightseeing bus is very expensive for what you get. The ride cost $40.88 for a 24 hour pass and $51.63 for a 48 hour pass. The bus only runs from 10:00 am to 6:00 pm. This wouldn't be bad if the bus actually went somewhere but it only runs up and down the Strip making 19 stops, mostly at the hotel tour lobbies (that are usually round back and off the Strip). There is a brief dialogue as you travel along but it's just not the same as taking a bus tour in London, Paris or Rome.

In time they may add more stops and venture off the Strip. But for now, you would be much better advised to spend $16 and get 2x24 hr. passes on the SDX or Deuce buses that run up and down the Strip and even go downtown. Save your money and give this one a miss.

3.3 What to do first?

There is always a lot of anticipation that comes along with going to Las Vegas. If it is your first visit you are wondering if you will hit it big and take home a fortune. After you've come a few times, your looking forward to seeing the things you missed last time and any new hotels/casinos that may have sprung up since your last visit. If you're a frequent visitor you already know what you like and what you're going to do..

In any event, once you get to the hotel and get settled in, there are a few things you could do to get the most out of your visit. Others may disagree with me, but here's what I suggest you do as soon as you arrive.

Decide on the shows you want to see

If you haven't already decided on the shows you want to see, sit down with the hotel concierge to get some suggestions on the shows and tours you may want to go on during your stay. The concierge will be able to tell you about what's hot and what's not. They can also tell you the prices and what days are dark (closed). But do not buy your tickets yet. Just get the information on the price, location and times of the shows and tours that interest you. Tell the concierge that you will need to think it over. A lot of show, tour and dinner tickets are discounted and we have already talked about this in *Finding The Best Discounts* section, so just be patient.

I think it is important to identify the shows you want to see at the beginning of your visit because the time will pass quickly and some shows and attractions are hard to get into or dark on certain days so you need as much flexibility as possible.

Get out and have some fun

By now, you're probably exhausted, so toss everything you picked up from the concierge onto the bed and get out and have some fun. You can decide later on the shows, tours and restaurants you want to experience and the best way to purchase your tickets. For now, this stuff can wait. Just get out and have some fun. After all, this is Las Vegas.

4.0 Shopping

Las Vegas is one of the great shopping destinations in the world. Ok, it doesn't have over 3,000 shops under one roof, like the Grand Bazaar in Istanbul or it doesn't get over a million visitors per day, like Myeongdong in Seoul, South Korea but it does have plenty of bargains and a great variety for everyone from the value shopper to the most discerning one.

No trip to Las Vegas is complete without some shopping.

So whether you are an ardent shopper, a bargain hunter or just into looking at what is in fashion in the high-end shops this chapter will take you on a short tour of what you can find in Las Vegas.

4.1 The Outlet Malls

There are two major outlet malls in Las Vegas. One is located on the north-end of the Strip and the other is on the south end of the Strip. Both outlet malls are on the bus route but they are not easily reached on foot. You will need to take some form of transportation to visit them. My preference is to take the bus unless you already have a car and don't mind driving.

Las Vegas Premium Outlets - North is located just minutes from the Las Vegas Strip, directly off the I-15 at Charleston Boulevard or two miles north of the Stratosphere. If you take the SDX express bus northbound it will drop you off and pick you up at the north end near the Ann Taylor and Disney outlets. You can also get there by taxi.

The mall has 150 stores (slightly more than the south outlet mall) and the hours of operation are the same: 10:00 am - 9:00 pm everyday except Sundays when it closes at 8:00 pm.

This north outlet mall is an outdoor mall so it can get hot in the summer, although the stores are air-conditioned. The mall has higher end stores than the south end outlet mall but many of the stores are the same. You can check out the stores and the map at:

www.premiumoutlets.com.

Just click on Nevada and pick the Las Vegas Premium Outlets - North.

My wife prefers the south-end mall because they seem to have better prices and we like the idea of being indoors in the hot weather. Although we do have many friends who prefer the north end mall because of the higher-end shops. You will have to decide for yourself once you check out the directories online.

The Premium Outlets are in most people's price range so regardless of which one you visit I know you will find something to fit your budget.

Las Vegas Premium Outlets - South is located just 2.5 miles south of the Strip with easy access from the I-15 via Blue Diamond Interchange. From the Strip follow Las Vegas Boulevard South to Warm Springs Road. If you take the SDX express bus southbound it will drop you off and pick you up at the north-end near Burlington Brands and Nike. You can also take a taxi.

The mall has 140 outlet stores and is open every day from 10:00 am - 9:00 pm except Sundays when it closes at 8:00 pm.

There are a large variety of shops with good value and good prices. The outlet mall is indoor so on a hot day it is very refreshing. You can get a map of the mall and a list of the stores at:

www.premiumoutlets.com.

Just click on Nevada and pick the Las Vegas Premium Outlets - South. The mall has two food courts and there are several restaurants just outside the mall if you want something more formal.

4.2 Town Square Mall

If you plan to visit the Las Vegas Premium Outlets - South then you might want to stop at the Town Square Mall on the way down or back. They are only one stop apart on the SDX express bus so it makes a lot of sense to combine the two stops on one trip. It will make for a long shopping day but what's wrong with that. After all, you are on holiday.

Town Square is designed as a European Village. It is an open air shopping, dinning and entertainment center developed on 117 acres.

Located between the Las Vegas Strip and Hwy 15, just south of Sunset Rd. (the southern boundary of McCarran airport) the mall can easily be reached by bus. Take the SDX express bus south on the Las Vegas Strip and get off at the Town Square stop. This is the stop just before the Las Vegas Premium Outlets Mall - South. If you are driving turn right off S Las Vegas Blvd. at Sunset Rd. and the Town Square will be on your left. Just follow the signs.

The village has over 1.5 million square feet of retail space and more than 150 stores to serve you. The village is a delight to walk through. In addition to the stores and dinning areas the village is family friendly and has a 9,000 square foot Children's Park. There is even an 18-screen movie theater.

The Town Square has a small town feel to it and most people find it very relaxing. It has quite a different feel to it than the Outlet Malls. It is usually not as crowded and most of my friends comment on how clean it is.

The mall is open 9:00 am - 9:00 pm everyday except Sunday when it closes at 6:00 pm.

For a complete list of the stores, entertainment and events you can go to their website at:

www.mytownsquarelasvegas.com.

you prefer to stay on the Strip there are an extraordinary number of premium shopping venues in the major hotel resorts. The following are my favorites but by no means all of them. Every major hotel will have a shopping venue but the four that follow are truly exceptional. Any trip to Las Vegas should include a visit to the first three; The Forum Shops, The Grand Canal Shoppes and The Miracle Mile.

4.3 The Forum Shops

Most people who visit Las Vegas will make a trip through the Forum Shops. Caesars Palace calls this the "Shopping Wonder of the World" and it is a must see. The venue occupies over 600,000 square feet (bigger than most Las Vegas casinos) with more than 160 shops and 11 gourmet restaurants there is something here for everyone. Pay particular attention to the crowd. This is one of the best celebrity sighting spots in Las Vegas.

You can enter from Caesars Palace or from the Las Vegas Strip. The shops are open 10:00 am - 11:00 pm, Sunday - Thursday and 10:00 am - midnight, Friday and Saturday. If you see one of the stores close its doors in the middle of the afternoon, it's probably because a celebrity is browsing inside.

Talking statues, an exotic fish aquarium and world-renowned restaurants. Oh, and the selection of high-end retail stores isn't too shabby either. With stores from famous designers like Salvatore

Ferragamo, Gianni Versace, Dolce and Gabbana and Louis Vuitton, you won't have a problem browsing. The Forum Shops also offers a nice blend of popular favorites. These include Guess, Gap, Express, Nike and the bargains at H&M.

The three-story H&M will blow your mind. With its energetic music, bright colors and stylishly-dressed mannequins suspended from the ceiling, H&M feels like a party and shopping spree rolled into one. Since it carries a wide selection of men's and women's apparel, no one will stand around bored while their significant other tries on clothes. If you shop wisely, you can probably put together an outfit with accessories for less than $100. That means more money to splurge on your trip.

Love chocolate and comfort food? Just across the way, Max Brenner - Chocolate by the Bald Man is a great place to take a break during your shopping spree. Where else can you find chocolate ranch dipping sauce for your fries and onion rings? In addition to a variety of creative concoctions like Choco-Pops (hot cocoa with chocolate wafer balls) and a strawberry white chocolate smoothie, you can enjoy savory bites, too. The food menu offers everything from panini and pizza to pasta and pancakes. Browse through the gift shop and bring some gourmet chocolate and the restaurant's signature "hug mug" home with you.

For those with a fancier appetite, the Forum Shops' selection of restaurants is sure to please the pickiest palate. These include Il Mulino New York, Spago, Sushi Roku, Joe's Seafood, Prime Steak & Stone Crab and The Palm, among others.

If you plan on walking through the entire mall, make sure to check out the 175,000-square-foot, three-level area featuring a spiral escalator -- one of only two in the country. Make your home fancy with a spree at Baccarat crystal. For edgier, hippie-style decor, Anthropologie offers plenty, along with bath products, accessories and vintage-inspired women's clothing.

Nearby, art lovers can stroll through Peter Max and Peter Lik galleries. Peter Max is known for his abstract, psychedelic art, while Peter Lik's claim to fame is his bright, digitally-enhanced photographs.

While you're in the exploring mood, see statues "talk" at the newly revamped Atlantis Fountain Show. These lifelike animatronic figures include a breathtaking fire and water show. The show runs every hour on the hour. While you're here, admire the 50,000-gallon aquarium featuring more than 100 species including stingrays, flounders, puffers and much more. Free below-the-scenes tours are available Monday through Friday at 3:15 p.m.

If you're in the hotel's casino area, make sure to check out the upscale shops at Appian Way as well.

The Forum Shops at Caesars Palace is owned and managed by Simon Mall. If you want to check out the sales and special events before you go, you can do so at the following web site:

www.simon.com/mall/the-forum-shops-at-caesars.

This site will give you a current list of the sales and special events that are available now and a complete list of the stores so you can spend more time shopping and less time looking for your favorite stores.

4.4 The Grand Canal Shoppes

The Grand Canal Shoppes at the Venetian is an outstanding shopping venue. Located on the second level (take the escalators just inside the front doors), it is reminiscent of walking the streets in Venice as they wind their way through a myriad of wonderfully dressed boutiques with something for everyone. Your stroll through this unique shopping venue is complete with a replica of the Grand Canal flowing along side the streets with bridges traversing the canal as gondoliers maneuver their gondolas while singing to the tourists enjoying the ride. Ok, a bit hokey, but what the heck, it is Las Vegas.

The Grand Canal and the blue sky painted ceiling make you feel like you are outdoors. The gondola ride lasts about 15 minutes and don't forget to kiss under the bridge, which I hear is good luck. Don't forget to kiss the one you're with, not the gondolier otherwise it could be very unlucky for you. Listen to the strolling minstrels and don't forget to look up into the balconies surrounding the piazza in the event a diva steps out to sing an aria from some well known opera.

The Shoppes are open Sunday to Thursday 10:00 am - 11:00 pm. On Friday and Saturday they open at 10:00 am and close at midnight. For a complete list of the shops go to:

www.thegrandcanalshoppes.com.

There are plenty of things to see and do besides shopping. At the end of your stroll along the canal you will enter a replica of Piazza San Marco. Spend some time here and just savor the atmosphere. If you are lucky enough to be here for one of the Carnevale di Venezia performances you will be treated to something special. Performances are at 1:00 pm, 2:00 pm, 4:00 pm, 5:00 pm and 6:00 pm every day. They run for 15 minutes and include opera singers, stilt walkers, dancers and "living statutes" that will take you to the very heart of Italy.

Give yourself enough time to leisurely wander The Grand Canal Shoppes. It's well worth the effort and a great place to be on a warm day.

4.5 The Miracle Mile

The Miracle Mile shops are a "re-creation of cutting edge trends and urbanized architecture that can only be described as out of this world". A bold statement by the mall manager but in this case it actually does live up to the hype. The architecture is a carryover from when the resort was the Aladdin. Expect to see middle eastern architecture blended with more modern styles in the theater district.

One of the highlights for me is the rainstorm that happens every day at the top of the hour from 10:00 am - 11:00 pm and every half-hour on the weekend. The best view for this is outside Tommy Bahama. If you are in the Miracle Mile make a point of seeing this, complete with thunder, lightning, fog and pouring rain. If nothing else, it will cool you down before going outside into the hot sun.

With 170 shops you are bound to find something that will interest you. If you want a complete list of the shops, dinning choices, current promotions and entertainment so you can be better prepared when you arrive, then check out the following web site:

www.miraclemileshopslv.com.

4.6 The Fashion Mall

With over 1.8 million square feet of space this is one of the largest enclosed malls in the world. The mall has over 250 stores, 7 anchor tenants (Dillard's, Forever 21, Macy's, Macy's Men's Store, Neiman Marcus, Nordstrom and Saks Fifth Avenue), an elevated stage, a fashion runway and "The Cloud". The mall has ten restaurants and a food court on the third level.

Fashion shows take place in the mall every Friday, Saturday and Sunday at the runway located between Saks Fifth Avenue and Nordstrom. Showtimes are on the hour from noon - 5 pm. If you arrive a little early you will get to watch the runway rise from the floor. It only comes out for the fashion show so don't miss it.

The Cloud is the saucer shape above the entrance. During the day, the structure provides shade for the entrance and in the evening it serves as a movie screen for promotion and important messages. It is quite spectacular to see at night.

If you want to visit the mall online for a list of stores, events and dining and entertainment information go to their web site at:

www.thefashionshow.com.

4.7 The LINQ

Located between the Quad and the Flamingo, the LINQ is an open air dining and entertainment district, anchored by the world's tallest observation wheel, the High Roller (550 feet). Higher than the London Eye (443 feet) and the Singapore Flyer (541 feet). It is a must see Las Vegas attraction.

The mall spans more than 300,000 square feet and features more than 30 unique retail, dining and entertainment experiences.

O'Sheas was one of the first venues to open, occupying space inside the Quad. O'Sheas has been on the Strip for 23 years before closing their doors in 2012 to make room for the LINQ.

Other venues include; 12AM:RUN, Bella Scarpa, Brooklyn Bow, Chilli Beans, Chayo - Mexican Kitchen, FRAME, Flour & Barley, Ghirardelli, Goorin Bros., KOTO, Polaroid FOTOBAR, Rubyblue, Sprinkles - cupcakes, The Tilted Kilt - Pub & Eatery, Vanity, Yard House and many others.

Every Tuesday night the LINQ has a block party. Go to the link below and then scroll down and click on the Block Party.

http://www.caesars.com/thelinq/.

4.8 Specialty Stores

In addition to the shopping venues described above there are a number of specialty stores that you might be interested in spending some time in.

Sephora is a visionary beauty-retail concept founded in France by Dominique Mandonnaud in 1970. Sephora's unique, open-sell environment features an ever-increasing amount of classic and emerging brands across a broad range of product categories including skincare, color, fragrance, body, smilecare, and haircare, in addition to Sephora's own private label. In Las Vegas there are three stores on the Strip at The Forum Shops, the Venetian and The Miracle Mile.

In addition to lip glosses, eye shadows and more mascara wands than you can imagine, Sephora also offers a wall's worth of designer fragrances for both men and women. You can also pick up some fun accessories like handheld mirrors, hairbrushes and compact mirrors.

You can check out their weekly specials, free samples and fragrance deals at their website:

www.sephora.com.

Ross Dress For Less is a nationwide discount chain where you can expect to find designer and brand name fashions for men, women, children and home at everyday savings of 20% - 60%. To keep their costs down they operate no frill stores with centralized checkout and simple fashion displays.

They are located at two locations on the Strip at 3001 S Las Vegas Blvd. (one stop south of the Riviera Hotel) and 3771 S Las Vegas Blvd. (at the Showcase Mall, just north of the MGM Grand). Both stores are on the east side of the Strip and they are open everyday from 8:00 am - midnight.

To find out more about the stores and what they carry, as well as what's in the stores now, check them out at their website:

www.rossstores.com.

These are just some of the shopping venues in Las Vegas that are close to the Stip. Of course every casino has shops and the higher end casinos, like Bellagio and Wynn have very high-end shops.

5.0 Spas

Las Vegas spas have no equal for sheer size and extravagance. Everything in Las Vegas is bigger than life and the spas are no exception. With over 45 spas on the Strip there is plenty to choose from. Over the years many of my friends and family have indulged themselves at the spa. If you just want to relax after a busy day of shopping, a long night of partying or you and some friends want to be pampered try one of these spas.

I have only included spas that offer day passes. Some of the hotel/resorts only allow guests to use their spas. If you are staying at a hotel on the Strip then check with the spa directly if it does not appear on the list below. As a hotel guest, you may be able to arrange your own appointment.

However, if it is not convenient for you to visit one of those listed below you can always go to one of the five star hotel/resorts nearest you and ask if they have a day pass. I am sure you will be able to find a world class spa you can visit in close proximity to you.

Canyon Ranch Spa at the Venetian

One of the largest day spas in the world is located on the fourth floor of the Venetian Resort with over 130,000 square feet, 82 treatment rooms, two cafés, a 40 foot rock climbing wall, a full gym, cycling studio and European technology like a water circuit called Aquavana, crystal steam rooms, experimental rain showers, a Finnish sauna, herbal laconicum and even an indoor igloo. Wow, need I say more.

Ok, but just a little more. The rest you will have to discover on your own. One of the spa's signature treatments is the Canyon Ranch Mango Sugar Glo, a body scrub derived from natural sugars, jojoba esters and betacarotene. You can check out the full menu at:

www.canyonranch.com/lasvegas.

Just click on MORE under Questions and Reservations, then download the SpaClub *Menu of Services*.

At Canyon Ranch you'll find a haven to relax, refresh and regroup between forays into the world's liveliest, nonstop city. You can take a fitness class, meet with a nutritionist or personal trainer and have a massage or facial. Aquavana, is their oasis of water therapies and includes state of the art hot and cold experiences.

The day pass costs $40 but it is subject to change. I suggest you call them, (877) 220-2688 to make a reservation and to get the most up to date information on any specials that might be available during your visit.

Qua Baths & Spa at Caesars Palace

In 2013 this spa, located inside the Augustus Tower, was ranked #28 out of the best 100 spas in the country, making it one of the best in Las Vegas. It offers 51 treatment rooms including three deluxe couples' studios and seven facial rooms. Amenities include a laconicum room, a herbal steam room, cedar wood sauna and whirlpool.

You can purchase a day pass for $45 giving you access to all their amenities. Since day passes can be suspended on very busy days it is best to check with the spas concierge, (866) 782-0655 before arriving.

The Qua Baths & Spa at Caesars is one of the city's newer spas and large at 50,000 square feet. It has a Roman Bath theme. In addition to the steam and sauna rooms, there is also an Arctic Ice Room to cool off in, although the man made snow looks suspiciously like foam. Cascading waterfalls and social mineral pools of varying temperatures invite guests into an aqua escape that's a treatment in itself.

Highly trained artisans perform a full range of treatments and wellness rituals including massages, Ayurvedic therapies, hypnotherapy and chakra balancing. There is something here for everyone. You will not be disappointed. Check them out at:

www.caesarspalace.com.

Click on *Things to Do* then on *Learn More* under Qua Baths & Spa for a complete list of treatments and prices.

Spa Bellagio

Spa Bellagio, located on the second floor, was the first truly extravagant spa to open in Las Vegas. Featuring a Zen influenced design that blends granite, travertine and jade surfaces with water walls and hand-blown glass decor. There are several tranquil lounge areas, juice bars and an open balcony overlooking the beautiful Bellagio conservatory.

With over 60,000 square feet and 56 treatment rooms, including four couples rooms, it's not just a spa: it's an experience. The salon is flashy with gold but the spa upstairs is quieter and earthier with nice touches like the jade tiles in the floor that are lit from below. The therapists here are uniformly wonderful, and it's one of the few places in Vegas where you can get a Watsu treatment.

Spa Bellagio offers a full complement of therapeutic and rejuvenating facial and body care treatments. One of the most popular massages at Bellagio is the A shiatsu, an ancient form of bodywork using deep compression. It is performed on a massage table by a barefoot therapist who holds on to bars attached to the ceiling. For a complete look at the their menu, check them out at:

www.bellagio.com.

Click *Explore Bellagio* and then select *Spa & Salon*. From here you can find a whole range of treatments and therapies.

You can purchase a day pass for $40 but like the other spas you should call ahead, (702) 693-7472 since these passes are subject to change, without notice.

Everyone needs that final bit of relaxation before heading back to the real world; so don't miss the spa's meditation room. Water walls surround the dim room, and candles provide a warm glow. A mix of New Age music and sounds of nature completes the soothing environment.

Paris Spa by Mandara

Founded in Bali, Mandara is a world-renowned retreat bringing its luxurious service to Paris, Las Vegas. By infusing sensual Balinese based health, beauty and massage techniques with the offerings of a continental spa, the staff provides an experience that sets itself apart from the rest.

Smaller than many of the spas on the Strip it offers a more intimate surrounding in the 26,000 square foot facility featuring handcrafted Balinese hardwood massage tables, imported embroidered silks and carpets, and artwork from around the globe. The 30 treatment rooms, six grand suites, a full service salon, cardio fitness center and a retail boutique featuring Elemis and La Therapies products also boosts an eucalyptus steam room, dry sauna, whirlpool, showers, lockers, vanity areas, relaxation lounge and cold plunge pool. This spa has it all.

You can check out their full menu and prices by visiting them at:

www.parislasvegas.com.

Then just look under *Things to Do* and scroll down to *Paris Spa By Mandara*. Click on *Learn More* for the full menu.

If you are not staying at the hotel you can still buy a day pass for $35 but check with the concierge, (702) 946-4366 before showing up since these passes are subject to change without notice.

The Grand Spa at The MGM

The Grand Spa is tucked away at the back of the property and the quiet, skylit pathway to the spa will make you feel like you are entering another world. With over 29,000 square feet decorated in warm, neutral tones with rock walls, wood accents and the Zen inspired themes there are 20 treatment rooms, private suites and couples treatment areas.

For a unique experience try the Nirvana. The treatment includes Ayuredic oils with an Abhyanga massage, Shirodara scalp treatment, hot stone placement, cool eye mask, copper bowl foot balancing treatment and warm foot wrap accompanied by customized music designed to give you the ultimate relaxation experience. If this doesn't do it for you, nothing will.

You can check out their entire spa menu at:

www.mgmgrand.com.

Just click on *Amenities* and then follow the link to *Spa*. When you are into the Services just click on the *Grand Spa & Fitness Centre* for Price List.

The spa gets high fives all around. With one of the warmest reception staff on the Strip, the hard part is choosing what you want and regretting you don't have more time.

They do not offer an all access day pass unless you are a guest of the hotel. However, you can make an appointment for a treatment, Monday through Thursday, as a non hotel guest and this will entitle you to a day pass for $25. To make a reservation call the concierge at (702) 891-3077.

The Spa at Encore
This is the first Forbes Five Star spa in Las Vegas. Located on the third floor of the hotel the 60,000 square foot facility opens into a large and spacious check in area. From here you have easy access to the spa, salon, fitness center and retail store. While waiting for your treatment you can relax in the den, just off the lobby or one of the luxurious quiet lounges for men and women.

From your arrival you will notice the Moroccan and Asian architectural influences. It feels like stepping into a sultan's palace.

The signature butterfly motif is everywhere, on the furniture, in the carpets and even hand woven in silk and affixed to the domed ceiling. The only word needed to describe the setting is opulent. Like everything at Encore the spa is truly a stunning combination of opulence and good taste.

The spa has 51 treatment rooms including 14 garden suites and two movement studios offering spinning, yoga, Pilates, conditioning and meditation for groups and private instruction. The spa offers a full range of treatments that you can check out at:

www.wynnlasvegas.com/Activities/Spas/EncoreSpa.

Just click on the *Encore or Wynn Spa* and then click on the corresponding Spa Menu to get a current list of the treatments and prices at each spas.

If you can't decide what treatment to have try the *Good Luck Ritual,* a 50 minute fusion massage, Thai herbal massage pillows, a peppermint foot treatment, an ultra moisturizing hand therapy and a wild lime botanical scalp treatment. The ritual is based on the five elements of feng shui to help achieve health, wealth, prosperity, happiness and harmony. If you are not relaxed after this 80 minute treatment you might need a little extra medication.

As a non hotel guest you can buy a day pass for $40 but check with the spa, (702) 770-4772 before showing up since these passes are subject to change without notice. If you sign up for a treatment worth more than $75 the day pass fee is waived.

The Spa at Mandarin Oriental

Located in CityCenter the spa is probably the most intimate, opulent and expensive spa in Las Vegas. With over 27,000 square feet of space it is one of the smaller spas on the Strip. Spread over two floors it was designed to evoke 1930s Shanghai. The facility has 17 treatment rooms, seven couples suites, a Chinese foot spa, relaxation lounges, steam rooms, a hammam, a laconicum, vitality pool, saunas and an ice fountain.

You can check out the complete menu at:

www.mandarinoriental.com/lasvegas.

Just click on *Spa & Wellness* in the banner. Click on the Spa Brochure for a complete menu with prices or just browse through the offerings.

If you are having trouble picking out a treatment, Try the lemongrass foot bath, a signature health treatment and spend the rest of the day floating between the vitality pools, the heat-controlled tepidarium (heat controlled) chairs and the ice fountain.

If you book a treatment with them a complimentary day pass is included. If you are not a hotel guest you can purchase a day pass for $80 (Monday to Thursday) or $90 (Friday to Sunday). You can call them, (702) 590-8886 to make a reservation.

6.0 Tours

There are many excellent tours that can be taken from Las Vegas and the surrounding area. The following are tours I have personally enjoyed and would have no hesitation recommending to family and friends. Where possible I will tell you the best time of year to take a particular tour although most of these can be taken at any time of the year, some are best seen at certain times. This list is in no particular order. Prices will vary depending on where you get your tickets. Wherever possible I have included a web site you can visit for current pricing information.

6.1 Desert Bloom

This is one of my favorite tours. Although there are desert blooms throughout the South West I will only comment on the one in Nevada with particular emphasis on Death Valley. This usually doesn't appear in most tour books and I doubt that you will find it in any of the hotel brochures either but if you are adventurous and manage to be in Las Vegas when the conditions are right, you will see a sight that will keep you captivated for a lifetime.

I saw my first full desert bloom in 2005, probably the best bloom in a century and you can't believe the feeling when you drive down a desert road, barren on both sides in the morning and yet filled with wildflowers in the afternoon, so thick that you would have trouble walking through them. This is something I will never forget.

There are over a 1,000 plant species in Death Valley National Park, including 13 species of cacti and 23 endemics (plants that are known to grow only in the Death Valley region). A good wildflower year depends on at least three things;

• Well-spaced rainfall throughout the winter and early spring,
• Sufficient warmth from the sun and
• Lack of drying winds.

Generally speaking, rains that are evenly spaced throughout the winter and into the spring will bring out the best blooms. You can track the conditions in real time at:

www.desertusa.com/wildflo/wildupdates.html.

There is also an excellent book, Desert Wildflowers Field Guide that you can buy from Amazon for Kindle, iPads and Smart Phones for just $4.99.

There are also some excellent pictures of the bloom on the site so you can see what it looks like before you go.

Peak Blooming Periods for Death Valley are usually:

• Mid February to mid April at lower elevations;

Best Areas: Jubilee Pass, Highway 190 near the Furnace Creek Inn, base of Daylight Pass.

Dominant species: desert star, blazing star, desert gold, mimulus, encelia, poppies, verbena, evening primrose, phacelia, and various species of cacti (usually above the valley floor).

• Early April to early May at 2,000 - 4,000 ft. elevations;

Best areas: Panamint Mountains.

Dominant species: paintbrush, Mojave desert rue, lupine, Joshua tree, bear poppy, cacti and Panamint daisies.

• Late April to early June above 4,000 ft. elevation;

Best areas: High Panamints.

Dominant species: Mojave wildrose, rabbitbrush, Panamint daisies, mariposa lilies and lupine.

There are no formal tours to see a desert bloom so the best way to explore it is to rent a car. My preference is to combine this trip with a drive into Death Valley.

6.2 Death Valley

Death Valley NP is one of the largest national parks in the country. The park itself is over 3 million acres and the valley is over 120 miles long so you won't see it all in one day. It is therefore important to plan your visit.

There are many excellent tours through the park. Pink Jeep Tours is one of the best. They are not the cheapest but their tour guides are well trained and very knowledgeable. The Jeeps keep the party small – usually 6 – 10 people. Rates are about $240 per person but you should go to their site at:

www.pinkjeep.com

for current rates and book online for any discounts that might apply. Just click on *Las Vegas,* then click on *Las Vegas Tours & Reservations* and scroll down to *Death Valley National Park* for the details.

You might want to go cheaper and rent your own car. I've done both but you will get a lot more information with a tour guide. However, if you do decide to drive watch for small tour groups when you stop and listen-in to the guide. This is not as good as having your own guide but you will get information you otherwise wouldn't have.

Also you will need to know that the desert and Death Valley in particular can be very dangerous at any time of the year. You do not want your car to break down in Death Valley. If it does, don't leave the car and wait for help. You also need to make sure your cell phone will work. Many spots in Death Valley have no service. You should also know that at any sign of rain you will need to head up as quickly as possible. Even the smallest amount of rain can cause a flood.

If I haven't scared you enough and you still want to do the drive yourself here are a few of my favorite spots to stop;

• Dante's View,
• Furnace Creek,
• Devil's Golf Course,
• Badwater Basin (the lowest point in the Northern Hemisphere),
• Scotty's Castle and
• Artist's Palette.

The drive from Las Vegas to Death Valley can take between two and three and a half hours depending on the route you take and the traffic conditions. The following web site:

www.nps.gov/deva/planyourvisit

will describe the four most common routes from Las Vegas. All of these routes will lead you to the Furnace Creek Visitor Center, your starting point for your tour.

6.3 Valley of Fire

Nevada's oldest State Park, the Valley of Fire, is located only 50 miles from Las Vegas and makes for an easy half-day excursion.

Unlike Death Valley this tour can be done without a guide. The Visitor Center offers excellent material to explore the Park. The 13 mile scenic loop will take you past many unique rock formations carved from petrified sand dunes sculptured into amazing shapes and contours by the wind, water and time (such as Rainbow Vista, Atlatl Rock and Fire Canyon). You will also see rich vibrant colors of sandstone and rare 3,000 year-old petroglyphs.

If you don't want to drive yourself, tours to the Valley run about $130 and you can book online with Pink Jeep Tours at:

www.pinkjeep.com.

Just click on *Las Vegas*, then click on *Las Vegas Tours & Reservations* and then scroll down to *Valley of Fire* for the detail.

6.4 Red Rock Canyon

Located just 18 miles (25 minutes) from Las Vegas, Red Rock National Conservation Area also has a 13 mile scenic loop drive. You will pass by the impressive Wilson Cliffs, the colorful sandstone Calico Hills, Indian roasting pits and pictographs at Willow Springs.

If you don't want to drive yourself, tours to the Valley run about $80.

The best price performance tour can be booked online with Casino Travel & Tours (a Vegas.com company) at:

www.vegas.com/tours.

6.5 Black Canyon River Rafting

This is an excellent way to spend a hot day in the summer. You can book this tour online with Casino Travel & Tours at:

www.vegas.com/tours.

Click on *Colorado River Tours* and scroll down to *Black Canyon River Adventure Tour*. This 5 hour tour will cost about $100.

The Colorado River is a constant 56 degrees and you will be given a towel you can wet in the river to make sure you stay cool. A coach will take you to a loading ramp where a pontoon raft will take you slowly down the river (no rapids on this trip). The raft will stop for lunch on a beech and if you are so inclined you can take a quick dip in the Colorado. You will also be treated to a most unique and awesome photo opportunity of Hoover Dam – from below it and on the river.

There are plenty of opportunities to get wet as you drift down the river, particularly when you pass another raft. Don't be surprised if you are handed a pail to defend yourself as the other raft starts throwing buckets of cold water at you. It is best to go on a hot day.

6.6 Zion National Park

In my opinion, this is the third most picturesque national park in the country. Bryce Canyon and Cedar Breaks are prettier but all three are more stunning than the Grand Canyon (in my opinion).

To truly appreciate Zion you need to visit the park from the Utah entrance. It's 162 miles from Las Vegas (I 15 N) to Zion (Springdale entrance UT 9). The drive takes almost three hours. You can get the full directions from Google Maps (Las Vegas to Springdale).

Park your car in Springdale and take the free Springdale Shuttle into the park. You can then transfer to the free Zion Canyon Shuttle that runs from April though November:

www.nps.gov/zion/planyourvisit.

After you click on the website, click on *Shuttle System* to get the details.

The Shuttle makes eight scenic stops in the park. The Zion Canyon Shuttles are the best way to see the park because cars are limited to where they can travel.

Just get off the Shuttle at a spot you want to visit (all scenic stops are described in the park guide and are clearly marked) and pick up the Shuttle when you are ready to continue. They run about every 7 minutes so you shouldn't have too long a wait.

If you are physically fit, you have the time and you have come prepared then the best way to see and appreciate Zion is to walk one of the many backcountry trails that vary in length from 3.6 miles (my favorite) to 16 miles in length. Go to:

www.nps.gov/zion/planyourvisit

and click on *Things To Do* (opposite the icon of the person hiking), then click on *Backpacking* to pick the trail that best suites your interest level and skill.

All park visitors are required to purchase a recreational use pass upon entering Zion National Park. A private vehicle and all passengers pay $25, individuals entering the park pay $12 and both passes are good for seven (7) days.

6.7 Ethel M Cactus Garden

Only 15 minutes, approximately 10 miles from the Las Vegas Strip, the Ethel M Botanical Cactus Garden is one of the world's largest of its kind. Take Tropicana Avenue to Mountain Vista Ave. Turn Right (south) on Mountain Vista Ave. Take Mountain Vista Ave. until you reach the intersection with Sunset Road. Turn left (east) and follow the signs to Ethel M.

With over 300 species of plants spread over 4 acres the garden is open daily, 8:30 am – 6:00 pm. Live chocolate production hours vary, but are generally Monday - Friday until 3:30 pm. Chocolate factory workers are not available on Saturdays and Sundays.

It is an easy walk, lots of shade and if it gets too hot for you just step into the factory to cool off and check out the chocolate.

7.0 Entertainment

Over the years I have learned that what makes a good trip great are not those things that you always do on any trip, such as gamble in Las Vegas, visit the Vatican in Rome or the Eiffel Tower in Paris but those unique things that take you out of your comfort zone and leave you with something special. This does not mean that you have to sky dive or bungee jump. It can be as simple as buying something that reminds you of the visit, taking a gondola ride at the Venetian or seeing a great show.

If you want to check the shows out before your visit there are a few sites on the Internet that I often use, including a complete list of all shows that gets updated daily (it is sorted by hotel but you can still get a good idea of what is available in the area you are staying in):

www.lvol.com/lvoleg/lvshows.html.

You can buy tickets from the hotel concierge – this is probably the most expensive way to buy a ticket or you can go the theater box office – the next most expensive way to get a ticket. My preference however, is to buy a discounted ticket – same seat but at 50% or more off the list price. If you skimmed over the section called *Finding The Best Discounts* then now is the time to go back and read it more carefully.

Las Vegas is the entertainment capital of the world. At any given time there are literally hundreds of shows to choose from. These can be categorized as; Production Shows, Adult Shows, Magic Shows, Headliner Shows, Comedy Shows, Tribute Shows, Hypnosis and Psychic Shows and Afternoon Shows.

Everyone's taste will be different but the shows below are my picks. I have seen all of these shows and attractions and would not hesitate to recommend any of them. I have seen a lot of other shows and attractions that I would not recommend to anyone but that's another story. If you do not have a personal preference and you have no idea what to see, you can always choose from my favorites.

Production Shows

These are big budget shows that generally stay around for many years. So don't worry if you miss one, chances are very good it will still be here the next time you visit.

Two production shows by Cirque du Soleil however are being revamped. Zumanity and Love are both getting an overhaul. Zumanity at New York - New York has been running for ten years and the face-lift should be ready by mid-2015. Love will take a little longer to overhaul and will not be ready until 2016.

The following are my favorite Production Shows. I hope you enjoy them.

O – showing at the Bellagio, see a preview at:

www.cirquedusoleil.com/o.

This is considered by many as the best Cirque du Soleil performance in Las Vegas and a must see event. You will not be disappointed and because the show is sold out for most performances you should get your tickets as early as possible. You also do not see these tickets discounted very often so be prepared to pay more than most of the other shows, but believe me, it is well worth the price. If this is the show you want to see go to the box office in the Bellagio and ask for the 10:00 pm show. This is the late show and through the week these tickets are discounted 25%. Try to get a seat in the side balcony (not the main balcony) but along either side. These seats are in a single row – no one is sitting in front or behind you. You will be right at the rail and you will be able to look down on the action. Try to pick your seats in the middle of the row if you can, although any seat in the side row will be good.

Mystère – showing at TI, check it out at:

www.cirquedusoleil.com/mystere.

It is one of the first Cirque du Soleil shows to premier in Las Vegas. Click on the preview to see if this appeals to you. I have seen this performance several times and of all the Cirque Du Soleil shows it reminds me the most of a circus. If you have children with you, this is an excellent show to see.

KA – another Cirque du Soleil performance and showing at the MGM Grand:

www.cirquedusoleil.com/ka

is also excellent. Check out the preview. In fact, this is my favorite Cirque du Soleil show. I enjoyed it even more than O. The staging alone is extraordinary and you will be amazed at how creatively they use the stage. The action takes place all around the theater so you cannot help but feel like you are in the action.

Menopause The Musical – showing at Luxor:

www.luxor.com/entertainment/entertainment_menopause.aspx

is a lot of fun if you are in the right age group. The cast of four women shopping for lingerie at a Bloomingdales sale sing 25 songs about chocolate cravings, hot flashes, loss of memory, nocturnal sweats and sexual predicaments. The lyrics parody popular baby boomer music, with notable numbers including "Staying Awake" and "Puff, My God I'm Dragging". Everyone is sure to get a laugh from this performance. Even the guys will enjoy it.

Recycled Percussion - playing at the Quad (formerly the Imperial Palace) is a small production show for those who are into "junk rock". Upon admission to the show the guests are offered a drumstick and a pot so they can join in on the highly interactive performance. The group placed third on America's Got Talent and is going into its fourth year in Las Vegas. If you want a highly charged, energetic show this is one of the best in Vegas.

Did I mention that I got my tickets from Groupon for $18.75 a person (over 70% off the general admission price). These guys are some of the best drummers you will ever see. Check them out at:

www.recycledpercussionband.com.

Adult Shows

These are also Production Shows but they are more suited for a mature audience.

Jubilee – showing at Bally's:

www.ballyslasvegas.com/shows.html

is my favorite all time Las Vegas show. It has been a classic Las Vegas showgirl show for over 30 years. I have seen it many times and while they continue to make changes to it the major production numbers, like sinking the Titanic and watching the story of Sampson and Delilah are still in every performance. But be aware, there is nudity in the evening show (although tastefully done) but they also offer an earlier family show. Tickets are moderately priced. Check out the 24/7 Magazine as they often have 2-for-1 ticket coupons.

If you decide to see Jubilee or even if you don't, there is a backstage tour that you shouldn't miss. Check out the details at:

www.ballyslasvegas.com/things-to-do.html

just click on Jubilee Backstage Tour Learn More.

It is offered at 11:00 am Monday, Wednesday and Saturday for $19.50 ($14.50 if you purchase a ticket for Jubilee). It takes 60 - 75 minutes to complete and your host is one of the showgirls in the production. The women will love the detail as she shows you around the three stories below the stage and the men will love following the showgirl around. You will see the costumes (they throw nothing out) and meet the seamstresses; electricians and carpenters that make the show run smoothly. Your host will explain her job and how hard it is to run up and down the stairs wearing a 25-pound headdress (in heels) not to mention the fact that she also has to reapply for her job every six-months. There is something for everyone in this backstage tour, not to mention the makeup session done by a Jublilee showgirl. Sorry guys, this is just for the girls, but you do get to watch.

Magic Shows

Magic shows have always been a big hit in Las Vegas. They have been part of the Vegas scene from the start. One of the earliest magicians to hit Las Vegas was Carl Ballantine ("The Great Ballantine"). He played opposite Harry James, Betty Grable and Sammy Davis Jr. at the El Rancho Vegas in 1956. His vaudeville style comedy routine involved stage magic tricks that tended to go hilariously awry. He is credited with creating comedy magic and influenced generations of comics and magicians that followed.

There are excellent magicians in Las Vegas. David Copperfield and Chris Angle are just a few of the high end acts you might want to see. But the following are, in my mind, much better price performers. If you get a chance, see one of these shows.

Penn & Teller – showing at the Rio:

www.riolasvegas.com

is a classical magic show but with a twist. They explain how some tricks are done and show you how they prepare for others. The final act is the "double bullet trick" where they fire a gun at each other, the bullet breaking through a pane of glass and each of them catching the others bullet in their teeth (a trick that took them several years to perfect). If you like magic, you'll love Penn & Teller. Check out some of their routines by doing a browser search for: Penn & Teller YouTube.

Illusions - playing at the Riviera:

www.rivierahotel.com/las-vegas-entertainment/illusions

is an excellent magic show. Jan Rouven brings the show to life. He is entertaining and personable. For many of the numbers you will be asking yourself - how did he do that. It's family entertainment at its best and the show has something for kids of all ages. Check out some of his routines by doing a browser search for: Jan Rouven YouTube.

Gerry McCambridge (The Mentalist) - performing at PH in the V Theater:

www.vtheater.com

was nominated the "Best Magician in Las Vegas" and recently voted the "World's Best Entertainer" in his field. In 2009 Gerry was voted one of the "Top 10 Absolutely Have To See" shows in Las Vegas. His show is mystifying and you will truly be amazed at what he can discover in just a few moments with someone chosen at random from the audience. Gerry is the creator, executive producer and star of the original TV show The Mentalist that debuted in 2004.

Headliners

Headliners are usually in town for limited performances so the best thing to do is to check on who will be in Las Vegas during your visit. The following link:

www.casenet.com/concert/concertvegas.htm

will give you a complete list of whose performing, for how long and at what hotel. Remember to get your discount tickets at TIX4TONIGHT.

In addition to these headliners there are several superstars that have signed up for multi-year contracts. Celine Dione, Shania Twain, Rod Stewart and Elton John all have extended engagements at Caesars Palace.

Celine, the best selling female artist in history, has so many superlatives to her name that her show is a must see. Performing in the Colosseum every night except Thursday she puts on a spectacular performance.

Shania, the world's best selling female country artist of all time gives an outstanding performance at the Colosseum every night except Monday.

Rod Stewart is another must see show at the Colosseum. One of the most successful music careers of all time he gives an electrically charged performance. You will feel as exhausted as he does at the end of the show. When he is in town he performs every night except Monday.

Elton John, world-renowned songwriter, singer and performer is also performing at the Colosseum every night except Monday.

These are four of the best performers in the world and no trip to Las Vegas would be complete without seeing one of them. Check out the link above to find out when they are playing at the Colosseum, get a ticket, sit back and enjoy the show. These headliners rotate at Caesars so make sure you know when your favourite is performing.

Comedy Shows

Las Vegas is full of comedy shows. There is probably a high correlation between laughter, feeling good about yourself and spending money. The type of comedy a person likes is also personal and what makes one person laugh will not necessarily appeal to another. The best thing for you to do is talk to the concierge about what you find funny and let them recommend a comedy show for you. If, like me, you are looking for something that is not too off color or full of four letter words then you might want to consider Rita Rudner.

Rita Rudner – performing at Harrah's after a brief stint at the Venetian is returning to where she performed from 2006 - 2010:

www.harrahslasvegas.com

click on Shows and scroll down to Rita Rudner. She has a great rapport with the audience and her jokes are fresh, current and very funny. The show lasts for 1.5 hours and she often takes questions from the audience. You won't be disappointed. I've seen Rita a number of times and her material is always fresh.

Tribute Shows

There is always someone doing a tribute show in Las Vegas. If you are into this type of entertainment then I might suggest the following.

Legends In Concert – a Las Vegas mainstay has been performing on the Strip for over 25 years (the show, not necessarily the performers). They have a rotating cast so you never know who will show up on a given night. All of the performers are excellent. You will not be disappointed. The show performs year-round six nights a week and the venue changes from time-to-time but you can check out the current location at:

www.legendsinconcert.com/las-vegas.

You will see incredible performances by celebrity look a likes including; Elvis, Tom Jones, Shania Twain, Garth Brooks, Cher, Madonna, The Beatles, Rod Stewart and many others.

The Bee Gees - If you are a fan of their music then the 75 minute tribute show playing at Excalibur:

www.excalibur.com/entertainment/australian_beegees.aspx

is for you. You will undoubtedly be pleased by both the song selections and interactive nature of the show.

The Beatle Show performing at PH:

www.saxetheater.com

has been voted the "best Beatle Tribute Show in the world". Each performance is live (no lip-sinking here). The song choices are excellent. They have great voices and their instrumentals are every bit as good as the originals. They electrified the audience, people were dancing in the aisles and everyone was up and clapping by the end. If you only see one tribute show in Vegas make it this one.

Hypnosis & Psychic Shows

I have never been interested in these shows so I do not feel qualified to recommend one to you. However, if this is your thing, speak with the concierge and get their suggestions. Be sure you clearly understand the content of the show before you go. Some of these can be very risqué.

Afternoon Shows

There are a number of afternoon shows that are heavily discounted. As you walk up and down the Strip people will offer you tickets to see shows for free, all you have to do is buy a couple of drinks. If you just want to get out of the heat, have a few drinks and watch some good entertainment try one of these shows:

Nathan Burton: www.nathanburton.com at PH, or
Mac King: www.mackingshow.com at Harrah's.

In addition to shows, there are exhibits, countless lounge acts and a large number of attractions.

Exhibits

Bellagio Gallery Of Fine Art

They are showing an excellent exhibit of Faberge eggs here until May 25, 2015. I saw this exhibit a few years ago and it was awesome. If you are in Las Vegas before May 25, 2015 you must make an effort to see this exhibit.

Admission is $11 - $16 and the exhibits change regularly. Make sure to checkout the website at:

before you visit. Click on the Site Map (it's at the bottom of the web page) and look for the link to the Gallery Of Fine Art to find out what is currently showing. For security reasons there is a limit to the number of people who are admitted to this exhibit so buy your tickets early.

Antique Car Exhibit at the Quad

This is one of the largest collections (over 250 cars) of vintage automobiles in the world. It is located on the fifth level of the Quad. If you are a car aficionados or you just want to see a unique collection of vintage automobiles including those owned by presidents, dictators and gangsters then don't miss this one. They have spruced this up a lot from when it was in the parking garage at the Imperial Palace and they now offer you a headset (at no additional cost) so you can hear the narrative on the car but there is a charge to go in. Nevertheless, this is a good way to spend a hot day.

Mob Attraction at the Tropicana

This attraction is a mix between entertainment and museum. Using a mixture of artifacts, storytelling and technology the visitor is guided through a highly interactive journey of the world of organized crime. They are given a never before seen look into the personal lives of some of the most notorious mobsters. In this interactive journey you go face-to-face with the mob and make decisions that will determine if you become part of the "family". Highly entertaining.

Lounge Acts

There are lounge acts in almost every casino. Some of them are good and some of them are great. They are generally available in the evening and most of them are free. The best way to enjoy them is to go into the lounge, sit down, order a drink and wait to be entertained. You can stand outside (a lot of people do) but it is a lot more fun inside.

Lounge acts are posted on the first day of each month at:

www.insidervlv.com/entertainment/lounges.html.

This is a great site to go to before your trip so you can select the lounge acts that appeal to you and get the times they are available.

Two of my favorite lounge acts are described below.

The Dueling Piano Show seen nightly at New York – New York. Don't let the name fool you. Yes there are two baby grand pianos but the performers duel each other to see who will get to sing and play songs chosen from the audience. The audience chooses by leaving tips in the cup on top of the piano for the pianist they want to sing and play their song. The one who gets the most tips wins that round. Then they're off to another song. My favorite are the Pinegar twins, Kimberely and Tamara who play nightly (Tues. - Sat.) at 8:00 pm – 2:00 am. Check them out at:

www.insidervlv.com/twinsHarrah.html.

Big Elvis performing at The Piano Bar at Harrah's is a must see. Pete Vallee does an excellent job and you can see him at 2:00 pm, 3:00 pm and 5:00 pm Monday – Friday. Check out some of his routines by doing a browser search for: Pete Vallee YouTube.

8.0 Attractions

Many of the world's great cities are associated with specific landmarks. It is impossible to visit Rome without taking in some of the more than 900 churches that dot the landscape. You would be remiss if you visited Amsterdam and didn't stop in at one of its great museums. You can not visit Venice and ignore the Grand Canal. Las Vegas is no different. Instead of viewing churches or museums you will find it hard to avoid the casinos. Not necessarily as places to play casino games but as architectural wonders to be observed.

It should not come as a surprise therefore that many of the attractions in Las Vegas are related to casinos.

There are so many attractions in Las Vegas that it's hard to know where to start. Since my objective is not to list all of them but to point out those that I enjoy the most, the following is a list (in no particular order) of the attractions that I would not hesitate to recommend to my family and friends.

The Fountains at Bellagio

This signature attraction at the resort hotel/casino is probably the most popular attraction in Las Vegas. The fountains are a unique combination of water, light and music that sway and dance to opera, classical and Broadway tunes. There are about thirty different performances so make a point of watching them more than once. The best way to view these are to sit on the patio at Mon Ami Gabi in the Paris hotel/casino across the street from the fountains. I like to get there early – say 6:00 pm before the tables start to fill. Have a drink before dinner and wait until the sun goes down behind the Bellagio. The fountains run on the hour and half-hour from late afternoon until 8:00 pm. They then run every 15 minutes. The traffic on the Strip will tend to block your view from time to time, but it is still worth it. If you only have time to see one number then stop on the sidewalk in front of the fountains with everyone else and wait to be entertained. Remember not to stand on the north side (towards Caesars Palace) because that is the direction of the spray.

The Fiori di Como

Since you are already at the hotel to see the fountains just wander through to the hotel lobby and look up. This magnificent chandelier was fashioned by Dale Chihuly. It is the largest glass sculpture ever made. The art piece that took about 10,000 pounds of steel to support and almost 40,000 pounds of hand-blown glass (2,000 pieces) to create covers about 2,000 square feet of the ceiling. If you want to see more of his work visit his Via Fiori shops that outline the Conservatory and Botanical Gardens just off the Hotel Lobby.

The Conservatory and Botanical Gardens

Located just off the hotel lobby in Bellagio and after viewing the Fiori di Como walk into the Conservatory. It is a room fifty-five feet high crowned by a glass ceiling. The flowers are replaced every two weeks so they are always fresh. The room goes through a total redesign five times a year to create a theme that coincides with Holidays, Chinese New Year, Spring, Summer and Fall. There is a great café in the back corner of the Conservatory that I will talk about when we look at dining, so plan your visit around your mid-day meal.

The Art of Robert McDonald at Bellagio

Located in the "O" theater lobby, this area features a collection of over fifty sculptures, original drawings, serigraphs and lithographs by the most collected figurative sculptor in America. Many of his pieces depict performers in Cirque du Soleil.

Bellagio Gallery of Fine Art

Located just outside the Conservatory, the Gallery offers the finest examples of paintings, sculptures and other impressive works by some of the world's most influential and renowned artists. The exhibits change regularly. Check online or at the Gallery for the current exhibits. General admission is $15.

The Grand Canal

As you approach the Venetian from the Strip you will see its signature attraction – the Grand Canal. This replica runs for over ¼ of a mile winding its way through the resort hotel. You can take an authentic gondola ride (and yes the gondolier does sing). Catch the ride from inside the resort at Saint Mark's Square. My preference is to do this in the evening. You can buy the tickets in advance for a specific time. This gives you time to have dinner at one of the excellent restaurants in the Square and then follow it up with a romantic gondola ride.

The Artwork in the Ceilings

The very best of the Venetian for me is in its attention to detail. Walk in off the Strip and as soon as you enter the foyer look up. You will see a replica of Michelangelo's Sistine Chapel. As you wander through the hotel and casino continue to look up and see an abundance of Italian art replicas.

St. Mark's Square at the Venetian

This is a replica of the Plazza San Marco (St Mark's Square) in Venice. It has much of the detail of the original and if you are lucky you may be there when the opera singers appear from a balcony and break out into song. There are also entertainers that wander through the square throughout the day giving short performances. Don't miss the mime that looks like a statue.

The Forum Shops

The signature attraction at Caesars Palace is a walk through the Forum Shops with its outdoor theme and sky blue ceilings to give you the feeling you really are outside. The sky changes with the morning sunshine; the afternoon clouds that float by and the evening stars that twinkle. There are over 150 shops so take your time as you stroll along. You are best to enter the Forum Shops from the Las Vegas Strip. It will save you the time of walking through the casino.

The Fall of Atlantis

Located in the Forum Shops the fountain show uses lifelike animatronic figures to recount the myth of Atlantis. As the story unfolds King Atlas tries to determine which of his children will rule Atlantis. The siblings try to destroy each another, poisoning the kingdom with their greed. Finally, the gods decide to step in and settle the dispute, launching the Fall of Atlantis. A 20 foot winged beast appears from behind Atlas' throne and watches over the destruction as Atlantis is consumed by fire and then flooding water. Surrounding monitors add to the drama of the show with a variety of visual displays. Be sure to get to the show a few minutes early to grab a good spot; the area gets crowded quickly.

The Saltwater Aquarium

Once the Fall of Atlantis show concludes, take a walk behind the fountain and check out more than 100 species of ocean life in a 50,000-gallon saltwater aquarium. You can watch as a diver feeds the aquarium's inhabitants (including puffers, flounder and sharks) each day at 1:15 pm and 5:15 pm. A second staff person is present during feeding times to answer any questions you might have. In addition, tours of the aquarium's facilities are offered Monday through Friday at 3:15 pm. A feature presentation is held every half hour from 11:30 am.

The Festival Fountain

The Fountain in Caesars Palace is guarded by four animatronic statues of Roman notables, who on the hour from 11:00 AM talk about the days of the Roman Empire. The production generated a lot of excitement when the center opened in 1992 but has lost some of its luster. Nevertheless, if you happen to be going by near the hour you should wait to see it.

The Atrium at Luxor

Luxor has the largest indoor atrium in the world. Thirty stories high and measuring 29 million cubic feet it can comfortably hold 13 Boeing 747 aircraft. Check out the inclinators (elevators running on an angle) that run at 39 degrees taking guests to their rooms.

Observation Deck at the Stratosphere

Standing at 1,149 feet the Stratosphere Tower is the highest freestanding tower in the United States. The Observation level at 869 feet is enclosed in glass and gives you a full 360 degree view of the Las Vegas Strip. The best time to go is in the evening. Others may tell you that they liked the Eiffel Tower view better but that was before they enclosed their observation deck with wire mess (for security reasons) making it virtually impossible to see anything and you can forget about taking pictures. The Stratosphere is out of the way but the best view by far. You won't be disappointed.

Extreme Rides

If you want the thrill of your life and you have the stomach for it, the rides at the top of the Stratosphere Tower are possibly the best you will ever experience.

Big Shot that carries you up a 160 foot mast in 2.5 seconds and then drops you to free fall and bounce up and down the mast three times before coming to rest. Experience a gut wrenching four g's on the way up and negative g's on the way down.

Insanity is a swing ride that extends 68 feet over the edge and spins passengers up to 40 mph at a 70 degree angle which will tilt your body onto one position - straight down. If you can keep your eyes open you will get a breathtaking view of downtown Las Vegas at over 900 feet above the ground.

X-Scream sits on a 69 foot roller coaster track that teeters taking you up until the track pivots and then dropping you back down the other side until you come to a sudden stop 900 feet above the ground. Just make sure you have a good, strong heart before you go on any of these. This is not your typical kid's teeter-totter.

Sky Jump is one of the premier tourist attractions in the world. It provides the highest controlled free-fall in the world. You plummet 855 feet or the equivalent of 108 floors.

You can check all of these rides out at:

www.stratospherehotel.com/Tower/Rides

before you go. This site will also have the current prices for individual and bundled rides.

Voodoo Zipline is one of the newest extreme rides. It is also one of the best. Located at 490 feet above the ground the zipline runs from the 51st floor of Rio's Masquerade Tower to the Ipanema Tower and back. A distance of about 1/3 of a mile. You travel at 35 mph and the ride takes about 45 minutes to complete.

The ride experience begins with check-in on the second level. You then take the elevator to the 51st floor where you get in line and wait your turn. Any loose items, flip flops, change etc. will be stored in a locker and picked up when you return.

Two people sit on each bench seat (it looks a lot like a double chair lift without the snow). The only thing holding you in is a lap strap. They do pull it tight.

The next few moments are the worst. They are absolutely terrifying. You are sitting with your back to the Strip waiting to be released. Suddenly you're off.

If you are into extreme rides you may want to give this one a try.

The Fremont Street Experience

The attraction is a 90 ft. high and 1,500 ft. long (four city blocks) canopy that covers the pedestrian mall on Fremont Street. Over 12 million lights cover the canopy and when synchronized with music produces a dazzling show of color and sound that is unique. There are also two sound stages on Fremont Street where bands give free concerts. The easy way to get here from the Strip is to hop on the northbound Deuce and go to the end of the line. It's just a short walk from here to the attraction. The light show starts at dusk.

The recent expansion to include a 12-story slot machine inspired zip line called *SlotZilla* lets you zip under the canopy (1,750 feet long) at 77 feet above the ground. A higher *Zoomline* at 114 feet will zip people in a horizontal position (like a superhero) just under the peak of the canopy at 40 mph. If this is something you would like to try I recommend you try it in the evening. It is awesome under the lights.

The Volcano at Mirage

This attraction was done over completely in 2008. Mickey Hart (legendary drummer for the Grateful Dead) teamed with Indian tabla sensation Zakir Hussain and Fountains of Bellagio design firm WET to create the all-new audio/visual spectacle. Don't stand too close to it when it goes off. You can feel the heat from across the street. Eruptions start at 7:00 pm and run on the hour until 11:00 pm.

Siegfried & Roy's Secret Garden and Dolphin Habitat

Located in the grounds behind the Mirage, this is an exceptional place. You come face to face with exotic and majestic creatures including white lions, white tigers, leopards and panthers. The dolphin habitat includes a large family of bottle nose dolphins. The grounds are open daily from 10:00 am to 7:00 pm but hours can change due to special events. They also have a trainer for a day program where you can go from tourist to dolphin trainer in a few hours and getting to participate in hands on activities, in the water with the dolphins. How cool is this. Follow the signs to the Secret Garden and Habitat where you can purchase tickets.

Sirens at TI

Located next to the Mirage is TI. The free Sirens show follows the story of how a band of pirates become enchanted by sirens and are lured into their cove. The ensuing clash between the sirens and pirates as they try to escape is told in song and dance. Performance starts at 5:30 pm and run every hour and a half until 11:30 pm except in inclement weather.

The Eiffel Tower

This is the main attraction at the Paris hotel/resort, if you don't count the food and fabulous French pastries but I digress. The tower itself is a half scale, 541 foot tall replica of the original. The best time to go up the tower is in the evening. You will get a good view of the Strip and the lights but don't expect to take too many pictures. The observation deck is covered in mesh so it is hard to get a clear picture.

The High Roller

This is a must see Las Vegas attraction. The High Roller is the world's tallest observation wheel at 550 feet. It is higher the the Singapore Flyer and the London Eye. It has 30 large pods that take 30 minutes to make one revolution. The pods do not shake or spin. They are stationary but do tilt to keep them level while the wheel is turning.

The pods move at a rate of one foot per second and each pod will hold 40 people. They never stop moving so walk along side the pod and step on briskly when instructed to do so.

The cost of the ride, that lasts 30 minutes, will be $30. It will give you an awesome view of the surrounding area looking to the north and south, parallel to the Las Vegas Strip. The attraction is the anchor client for the new outdoor shopping, dining and entertainment mall called The LINQ.

The LINQ

With over 30 venues, this outdoor mall runs between the Quad and Flamingo (down what was once a driveway) leading up to the High Roller. There is over 300,000 square feet of retail space. So everyone should find something interesting.

Remember to check out The LINQ on Tuesday evening when there is a regularly scheduled block party. Happy hour, reduced drink prices, free outdoor entertainment and numerous discounts. Currently the High Roller is at half-price for locals (anyone with a Nevada drivers license).

9.0 Dining Out

There are many fine restaurants in Las Vegas and depending on your taste you can be sure to find a number of them to fit your criteria. Check out the following site for a complete list of all restaurants in Las Vegas:

www.lasvegas-nv.com/restaur.htm.

Alternatively, the concierge at your hotel would be pleased to work with you to identify a restaurant to fit your budget, cuisine, atmosphere and location.

In this chapter I would like to focus on the places that I like to eat. If you haven't already made a choice, then try one of these. They are all moderately priced, have a good selection to choose from and offer excellent food. While most of them have interesting décor my primary reason for recommending them is the quality and value of the food. Enjoy.

Buffet Discounts

Before we get into the detail I have to say a few words about buffet discounts. When I first came to Las Vegas in 1984 buffets were highly subsidized as a way of attracting people but as the economy worsened the subsidies shrunk (funny how that happens). However, as attendance also declined the resorts realized that they did need to do more to get people back to their properties so they started introducing food discounts.

Most of the large gaming companies now offer 24 hour buffet discounts across their properties. The average breakfast buffet today will cost you between $15 to $20 plus, lunch buffets can run from $20 to $25 and dinner buffets are $30 plus.

Caesars Entertainment has the Buffet of Buffets Pass that can be used at their seven properties: Bacchanal Buffet at Caesars Palace; Le Village Buffet at Paris; Spice Market at Planet Hollywood;

Paradise Garden Buffet at the Flamingo; Flavors, The Buffet at Harrah's; Carnival World Buffet at the Rio and Emperor's Buffet at the Quad. You can eat at any or all of these properties as often as you wish within a 24 hour window. Alcoholic drinks are extra. The price is about $55 ($5 less if you have a Total Rewards card). It is worth your while to sign-up for the Total Rewards card before buying the pass. If you do have a Total Rewards card you can show the card to get the 24 hour access, otherwise they will give you a wrist band that will get you access.

You will have to pay a premium (about $20) if you want to include Caesars Palace. Since most of us will probably have a hard time eating at multiple buffets in 24 hours, it does become important to strategize on how you're going to do this. I like to eat dinner a little latter on the day I purchase the pass, this allows me to get in a breakfast, lunch and dinner the next day. Eating four meals with the pass drops the average price per buffet to about $12.50. This makes the pass an excellent value. Believe me, you will be glad to see the end of the buffets after the fourth meal. If you use the pass at the beginning of your trip you will still have time to lose some of the weight you will invariably gain at the buffets. It's funny how quickly you can put the weight on but how long it takes to get it off.

Since the Bacchanal Buffet at Caesars is arguably the best and most expensive one in Las Vegas I would encourage you to eat at least one meal there (preferably a dinner), more if it is convenient. You could then have breakfast at the Paradise Garden Buffet (Flamingo), Lunch at the Spice Market (PH) and a dinner at the Le Village Buffet (Paris). If you don't want to pay the premium for Caesars buffet then have your first and last dinner at the Paris buffet.

Luxor offers the all day buffet pass for $35. Enjoy the The Buffet at Luxor all day for the one low price. Tickets can be purchased at the buffet.

Just remember, not all buffets are the same. Some are very high quality like, Caesars Palace and Wynn while Paris (my favorite) is a notch below. Others, like PH, Mirage, Harrah's and the Flamingo are a good second choice. However, I would never eat at the Emperor's Buffet, Circus Circus and the Rio (which I think is highly over rated, but that's my opinion). The last time I went into the Emperor's Buffet it was empty. I can still remember my mother's advice inside my head as we quickly turned and ran out (never eat at a restaurant that is empty, it is empty for a reason). Besides, the food isn't turning over fast enough to stay fresh.

Breakfast

Let's start with the first meal of the day. If you're like most people who visit Las Vegas the chances are good that you will not get out of bed until well after the sun has risen. You probably also want something quick to go with your coffee to kick start the day. I don't know many people who want to stand in line for their breakfast so my preference is to make a quick stop at the nearest café and order a continental breakfast; muffin, bagels, coffee or orange juice. All of the Resort Hotels have excellent bakeries so you can always be sure that the food is fresh and tasty.

If you are an early bird and want to get off to a quick start, a stop at the gym or visit to the spa might be your preference. Most of the high end spas on the Strip have excellent cafés so you should have no problem getting a nutritious breakfast.

If you decide to stay at a timeshare you can probably bring in food for breakfast since you usually have a small kitchen with at least a microwave, toaster and fridge. The timeshare will probably have a concession where you can stock up milk, cereal, bread, eggs, fruit etc. to get yourself off to a good start.

If you are looking for a more satisfying dining experience for breakfast here are my suggestions.

Tableau (Wynn) is located off the Spa Tower reception area. You may have to ask for directions. It is situated in an airy, elegant rotunda overlooking the pool and offers a gourmet menu with five star service. The meal will set you back about $30 (excluding any breakfast cocktails) but for something truly different try the lobster and shrimp frittata with caramelized onions, creme fraiche and salmon roe. Not only is this possibly the best breakfast in Las Vegas but it may very well be the best breakfast you have ever had.

Bouchon (Venetian) is a replica of a high ceiling European café overlooking the Venezia Tower's secluded pool. Sit on the outdoor terrace and you will have a hard time believing you are in the American dessert. The breakfast menu is moderately priced with the most tempting dishes. My favorite dish is *Gravlax* (smoked salmon with a petite baguette, chive cream cheese, red onion, tomato and capers). But the *Bouchon French Toast* (bread pudding style with warm layers of brioche, custard & apples served with maple syrup) is a close second. In most cases you can have an outstanding breakfast for under $20.

Payard Bistro (Caesars Palace) is a small dinning room hidden at one end of his patisserie offering classic Gallic petit dejeuner made in a central cooking station. Try the chocolate French toast with Nutella, sautéed banana compote and whipped cream. It's to die for. Expect to pay about $20 for breakfast.

Lunch

There are many excellent places to have lunch. Where I eat, often depends on where I am at the time. These are my favorite places for the noon meal.

Pizza Place (Wynn) used to be called Sugar & Ice. It is a small café just to the left of the doors when you enter off the Strip. The sandwiches were excellent and the brownie was out of this world. This menu has now been replaced with pizza by the slice and some Italian sandwiches. The food is still good but the ice cream is excellent. Make sure you get a table on the patio so you can watch and listen to the waterfall as it cascades down the rocks into the pond below. Portions are a good size and the price is very reasonable. Leave room for some homemade ice cream.

Kahunaville (TI) is a tropical restaurant and a Las Vegas hot spot that offers delicious menu items from the islands like kon tiki coconut shrimp and pina colada chicken (two of my favorite dishes). They also have a wide range of signature frozen cocktails. If you want to be entertained get a seat near the bar because the bartenders (who have competed in competitions internationally) add acrobatic flair to mixology by juggling glasses and bottles while creating their legendary cocktails. You can expect to pay $20, without drinks.

Towers Deli (Venetian) makes great sandwiches. Try the New York Sky High; it's my favorite. The Deli is located on the second level just before you get to the food court. My wife and I usually share this very large sandwich and order a side of potato salad, bag of chips and a large drink. The sandwich comes with coleslaw and a dill pickle. It is an excellent sandwich. It's messy to eat but well worth the trouble.

Greenburg's Deli (New York – New York) is located in the Greenwich Village styled area of the resort where they even include real menus from New York Chinese takeout restaurants taped to the doors of the mock buildings. I particularly like the steam coming out of the fake sewers. It gives it that real New York smell, look and feel. Their sandwiches are fantastic.

Village Eateries (New York – New York) has a number of fast food places that serve excellent food and large quantities at a modest price. Check out the foot long hot dogs and while you're at it try an order of nachos with the works on it. You can split the hot dog, share the nachos and get a large drink for under $10. The atmosphere is authentic even down to the steam coming out of the sewers. If you're a native New Yorker you'll love it.

JJ's Boulangerie (Paris) is a small café located across from Le Village Buffet. Just follow your nose you can't miss it. It offers a superb selection of sandwiches. Try one on a croissant (the bread is made on site) and it doesn't even matter what the filling is.

Snacks (Bellagio) is located on the right just before entering the casino. They offer a wide selection of sandwiches and light meals. Try the Butter Chicken Wrap, to die for.

Café Bellagio is located in the back corner of the Conservatory. Guests gaze through turn of the century arched windows to superb views of the pool area and Botanical Gardens. It is upscale but the meals are moderately priced and the décor is excellent. Indulge yourself, you deserve it. My favorite lunch is the smoked salmon on a bagel.

Ping Pang Pong (Gold Coast) is located just off the Strip so it is a little harder to get to. Take the free shuttle from the north east corner of Flamingo Rd. and S. Las Vegas Blvd to the Gold Coast and Rio. You can walk through the parking lot to the Gold Coast. It serves dim sum from 10:00 am to 3:00 pm. The food is authentic and reasonably priced. If it wasn't for the fact it is in the Gold Coast you would think you were in China. If you like authentic Chinese cuisine you've got to try it. I like to go early, around 11:30 am. It is always crowded but definitely worth the wait. The lines move very quickly.

P. F. Chang's (PH) is on the Strip so you may want to have your Chinese food here instead of taking the shuttle to Ping Pang Pong. I like both restaurants so I make a point of eating at both of them. The dim sum menu at P. F. Chang's is very limited so I usually eat my dim sum at Ping Pang Pong. Nevertheless, P. F. Chang's cuisine is always fresh, contemporary and consistently outstanding. They have some excellent lunch specials. Sit on the patio in the shade and watch the world go by. Priceless.

Lobster Me (Miracle Mile) is located about half-way around the Miracle Mile so it might be a bit of a walk for you but it will be worth it. They have one of the best lobster bisques I have ever tasted. It is served in a bread bowl but it does make a great lunch. Try it with their Lobsicle (lobster tail, deep fried on a stick) served with drawn butter. A bit expensive but simply delicious.

Sweet Chill (Aria) is located on the second floor. The café has an ultra modern retro look, so it takes a little getting use to. The seats are all plastic but comfortable. The menu includes sandwiches, salads, coffee and gelato. It's not busy and service is very quick. You can get a great tasting lunch for about $10.

Dinner

Everyone wants to know about the Buffets, so let's get them out of the way first. Not all Buffets are equal and the quality does change over time. A lot of people are told that the Rio has the best buffet and that may have been true 20 years ago but I would not go there today. So be careful when people tell you about a great buffet always ask them when they were last there, it does make a difference. There was also a time when buffets were cheap. Not any more. Most buffets have become indistinguishable based on what they serve. The Buffets listed below are my favorites. I make a point of eating at them.

The Bacchanal Buffet (Caesars Palace) is probably the best buffet in Las Vegas. Recently opened after being closed for a year during renovation the buffet is a massive 25,000 square feet. It has seating for over 600 people and offers over 500 items daily. The food is excellent and the choices dazzling. Pace yourself, you cannot try everything in one sitting so you probably will come back again. If you only try one buffet during your visit, try this one.

The Buffet (Wynn) is one of the best buffets in Las Vegas. It offers a wide variety of cuisine from different countries around the world. The menus change regularly so make sure to check the posted menu to see what is being served on a given day.

Do you remember that I told you to get your Loyalty Cards as soon as possible after arriving? Well this is where the Wynn's Red Card comes in. Wynn sometimes has a promotion to induce people to sign up for the Red Card. Check to see if it is available during your visit. It works like this. Once you sign up for the card you have 24 hours to accumulate 150 points on the card. Remember, you can do this faster if two of your party use the same card, so make sure you ask for two cards and only one person signs up initially. If they will not give you two cards when you sign up, go back a little later and tell them you lost your card so you can get a second one. It shouldn't take you long to get 150 points, about an hour or so if both of you are playing (even on penny slots). When you have 150 points take it back and get two free buffet tickets to one of the best buffet in Las Vegas. The second person in your party can now sign up on another day and you can get two more free buffets. The dinner buffet is $30+ so getting 4 for free really adds up.

Le Village Buffet (Paris) is a soft spot for me because I love French cooking, I readily admit it and Le Village Buffet has long been a favorite of mine. Le Village Buffet brings to life different provinces of France through culinary expertise and visual attention to detail. Each station is themed for a particular province and features an intricate facade designed to replicate the architecture of that region. Meals are prepared as they are ordered to ensure the quality and freshness of each selection. A large selection of pastries, pies and an assortment of sugar free delicacies are offered from the buffet's dessert station. You'll dine in a village like setting, where you may choose to eat outside in the town square or in a casual dining room by a fireplace. Each province's cottage dining room is decorated for the region.

Try not to eat every dinner at a buffet. There are many other restaurants that you should try. If you are like me you will eat a large lunch and then have a smaller dinner. When the weather is particularly hot I prefer to have a salad for the evening meal while sitting around the pool. But, if you would rather go to a restaurant, here are my choices.

Le Café Ile St. Louis (Paris). I already told you I love French cuisine so this choice shouldn't be a surprise. Sit in the al fresco style courtyard overlooking the hustle and bustle of the casino floor. It's a great place to people watch while you have dinner. The food is excellent and while there isn't a large variety to chose from I always find something I really like. My favorite dish is coq au vin (braised in a red wine sauce with pearl onions, carrots and egg noodles).

Mon Ami Gabi (Paris) is a nice casual restaurant located just inside and to the left of the main doors into the casino. They have an outdoor patio that is a great location for watching the fountains at Bellagio. Try to get there early to get a good seat on the railing for the best view of the fountains. Have a drink before dinner and take your time if you want to enjoy the fountains. Just remember that the fountains run on the half hour until 8:00 pm and then every 15 minutes. The menu offers the finest grain fed midwest beef hand selected for exquisite marbling and unmistakable flavor served with their signature fries. They also serve several fish dishes as well as diner size salads. Everyone can find something here.

Café Bellagio (Bellagio) is located in the back corner of the Conservatory, guests gaze through turn of the century arched windows to superb views of the pool area and Botanical Gardens. It is up scale, bright with an open concept. The food it excellent and they offer a daily special for less than $20. This is one of my favorite places to eat. Try it. I know you'll like it.

The Grand Lux Café (Venetian) is operated by the Cheesecake Factory and there are two locations in the hotel/casino. The décor is inspired by the look and feel of classic Venetian cafés and its design is both intricate and intimate. The food is excellent. I particularly like the dinner salads. The Polynesian salad with fresh fruits is one of my favorites. The chicken potpie is also very popular.

Bonanno's New York Pizzeria - Restaurant - Bar (PH) is located on the Strip at 3717 S Las Vegas Blvd just outside PH. It is sandwiched between Walgreens and McDonald's on the south end of the block. The venue is small so go early to get a table but the food is excellent and well worth the wait. My wife and I always make a point of stopping here when we are in the area. The staff is friendly and attentive. They have an excellent selection of wines to complement their pasta and entrees. The baked ravioli is one of my favorites.

Snacks

If you are feeling hungry in the evening and you just must have a snack, you can always stop at any number of cafes in the hotel/ resorts along the Strip. There are eleven Starbucks locations on the Strip alone. You will find them at the following resorts; Ti, Mirage, MGM Grand, Bellagio, Caesars Palace, Stratosphere, Harrah's, PH and they also have three outlets in CityCenter. So wherever you are on the Strip you should be able to satisfy that craving.

However, if you are in your room and you don't want to pay the mini bar prices you could nip out and bring your snacks back to the room. Most casinos have a small variety store with high prices. You can buy snacks here but I wouldn't bother. You are much better advised to go out on the Strip and search out a CVS Pharmacy, Walgreens or ABC Store. They carry everything you are likely to need, including liquor and beer at very reasonable prices.

CVS Pharmacy has two stores on the Strip, one north of Circus Circus and another near Monte Carlo. They have a wide selection of pharmaceutical products but they also carry an extensive range of food and beverages. They have beer, wine, soft drinks and water (this is important in Las Vegas). They have milk, cheese, eggs, yogurt, spreads, bread, cereal and other breakfast food. You get the idea. Oh, I left out cookies, potato chips and all that other stuff we're not suppose to eat. Did I say ice cream?

Walgreens has stores at the Convention Center Drive on the Strip, at the Fashion Mall, Venetian and Monte Carlo. I don't find their selection as good as CVS but they do carry groceries and in a pinch they will do just fine.

ABC Stores are new to the Strip but they have some good locations, Fremont Street (1), Riviera (2), The Fashion Mall (1), and Miracle Mile Mall at PH (2). These stores have a good selection and excellent prices. They carry a wide range of breakfast food including muffins, juices, coffee and fruit.

10.0 Closing Remarks

I would like to thank you again for purchasing *Las Vegas Travel Tips*. I hope you enjoyed reading it as much as I enjoyed writing it for you.

If you liked the book and if it made your trip more memorable, allowed you to get around easier, helped you select a few good shows and dining venues, whatever the outcome, please take a few moments to write a review on Amazon. Reviews are important to an author because in many cases they are the only feedback we get. They can also be invaluable to others, like you, who are just looking to have a great Las Vegas experience.

I hope your trip is truly remarkable and you return to Las Vegas in the near future. Oh, just remember what happens in Vegas stays in Vegas but the weight you put on comes home with you.

Have a really great time.

Mike

About the Author

M. J. Veaudry holds a Bachelor Degree in Computer Science and a Masters Degree in Business Administration. He has held a number of senior management positions in the computer industry and was a partner with one of the world's largest professional services firms. As a management consultant he has worked in the US, Canada, Europe and Asia.

As a gaming aficionado he has had a long time interest in playing and betting strategies as they relate to casino table games and slot machines.

Mike has been visiting Las Vegas since 1984 and he has been a property owner here since 1994.

He is a fitness nut who travels extensively but admits freely that Las Vegas is his favorite city in the world; the place he loves to return to.

Other Books by M. J. Veaudry

If you enjoyed *Las Vegas Travel Tips* you might also enjoy reading one of Mike's other books, available in paperback and in electronic form on Kindle. Any combination of the three books makes a great companion set for anyone planning a trip to Las Vegas or if you are just looking for a gift for that hard to buy for person.

Mike's Guide to Better Slot Play is the number 1 selling book on *Slot Machines* on Amazon and has been in this spot since it was first released. It explains in simple terms how slot machines really work and using this information shows you how you can be a better slot player. Tired of losing at the slots and going home with empty pockets? Let Mike show you a process with rules and techniques for improving your slot play. A proven way to manage your money better and to make sure you leave with your winnings. Learn how to bet less and win more.

Praise for Mike's Guide to Better Slot Play

Jason C. Mortenson, Wausau, WI - This Advice Works
"Take it from a mathematician. The advice Mike gives in this book will definitely make you a better slot player... By using Mike's betting strategy, which is not difficult to do (there are no mathematical formula or anything), you will curb the odds a little more in your favor and greatly extend your playing time... Highly recommended for anyone who plays the slots on a regular basis."

Christine Moore, Timonium, Maryland United States
"I've always been a person to just play the money until it was gone. I never seemed to come home with money. A few new casinos opened up near my house and now I have the opportunity to play more. I decided I couldn't keep throwing my money away. I wanted to have the entertainment of the slots but not come home empty handed. I employed the techniques in the book at my next trip to the casino. It really worked! I actually came home with some of the casino's money for a change! Yeah me!"

Casino Games Demystified is written for people who would like to play casino table games but do not have the confidence to step up to the table. They watch people laughing and having fun at the craps table but they are not sure how to play the game. Roulette looks interesting but it is probably too complicated. There are several card games they could play but they are probably expensive so they watch for a while, but then move on.

If this sounds familiar, then Casino Games Demystified is a great little book for you. Only a hundred pages, easy to read, entertaining and witty. Find out about the fundamentals of table games and table etiquette. Learn a bit about the history, rules of play, and betting strategies of six popular casino games. There are even step-by-step instructions for each game to get you to the tables to play with confidence.

Praise for Casino Games Demystified

machines. I considered most of the table games in the casino complicated and way out of my experience level. Casino Games Demystified, not only entertained me, it familiarized me with a little gaming history, pointed out important rules to follow, and provided simple-to-understand strategies that gave me confidence. Veaudry's inclusion of websites where I could practice what I learned in the book for free was an unexpected extra bonus for which I am grateful. Look out Vegas!"

B. Mac, WA
"Understanding casino games. My wife and I travel to VEGAS twice a year (spring and fall). I also visit the local casinos probably 2 to 3 times a month. The Book was very informative and very easy to understand. I would only play Black-Jack and Slots, until I read Mike`s Book. Now I can go into a casino and have the confidence to walk up to a Craps table, PaiGow poker, etc. and understand enough about the game to get started. Casino Games Demystified is just a great book and would recommend it to a friend or anyone, anytime.

I also have Mike`s Guide to Better Slot Play, also an excellent book."

Carolyn Stewart, Cottage Country
"I have been to the casino and stood by the gaming tables but lacked the confidence to participate. If you ever wanted to join in the fun then this book is for you. It answers your questions in a clear, orderly manner which explains the game and gives you step by step directions. I selected two specific games and then went into action following all the strategy and hints. I appreciate that the author doesn't mislead you into expecting huge returns but gives sound advice on bankroll management and encourages the fun side of casino games."

9

CPSIA information can be obtained at www.ICGtesting.com
Printed in the USA
LVOW04s0240160115

423073LV00029B/1462/P